ARCHAEOLOGICAL ASSESSMENT OF THE SELLS VICINITY, PAPAGO INDIAN RESERVATION, ARIZONA

Prepared for

STRAAM Engineers, Inc.

by

Carol A. Coe

Submitted by

Cultural Resource Management Section
Arizona State Museum
University of Arizona

June 1979

Archaeological Series No. 131

ABSTRACT

In July 1978 STRAAM Engineers, Inc., contracted with the
Cultural Resource Management Section of the Arizona State Museum to
prepare an assessment of archaeological resources in the vicinity of
Sells, some 60 miles southwest of Tucson on the Papago Indian Reservation. An extensive review of literature on the Papaguería resulted
in a discussion of environmental factors, culture history and previous
research. A records check for the 12.75 square mile area around Sells
defined as the project area resulted in an inventory of 18 sites previously recorded by the Western Archeological Center, National Park
Service, Tucson, and by the Arizona State Museum. This inventory, in
conjunction with site specific data for the project area, was used
to identify archaeologically sensitive areas within the project
boundaries. Recommendations for survey and monitoring were made for
the areas to be affected by planned sewer facilities improvements. At
the conclusion of this report a long term inventory survey is recommended
for planning purposes.

ACKNOWLEDGEMENTS

Several individuals were of assistance in the preparation of this assessment. Henry G. Atha of the Papago Tribal Utility Authority (P.T.U.A.) and STRAAM Engineers, Inc., are thanked for their technical assistance. Mr. Atha's tour of Sells was especially helpful for developing the recommendations in this report. Larry Garcia, of the Papago Tribal Housing Authority is thanked for identifying housing lot locations not shown on current maps. John Clonts, Douglas R. Brown and Bruce Masse of the Western Archeological Center provided data from WAC files and unpublished manuscripts, as well as valuable comments from their archaeological experience in the Papaguería. Their patience with my lengthy questions is appreciated. Susan A. Brew (ASM) kindly reviewed areas she had previously surveyed within Sells and is acknowledged for her fine typing job. Ellen Horn, Assistant Curator at the Arizona State Museum, is thanked for her assistance with photographs in this report. John Bancroft edited the report. Most of all, I am grateful to Sharon S. Debowski, Project Director, for her careful review of the draft report, her thoughtful suggestions and her unfailing support.

TABLE OF CONTENTS

LIST OF FIGURES

LIST OF TABLES

CHAPTER 1

INTRODUCTION

In July 1978 the Arizona State Museum contracted with STRAAM Engineers, Inc., of Phoenix, Arizona, to prepare an archaeological assessment for a parcel of approximately 12.75 square miles in and around Sells, Arizona, on the Papago Indian Reservation. The primary purpose of this assessment is to provide data on known archaeological resources within the project area and to identify potentially sensitive areas, so that archaeological resources can be considered in any modifications of, or additions to, the existing sewer system in Sells. These data also are generally applicable to future undertakings receiving federal funding, subject to federal licensing, or on federal land within the project area. Thus this report is designed to fulfill the immediate planning needs of STRAAM Engineers, Inc., and to serve as the basis for long term development plans for the Papago Tribe within the 12.75 square mile parcel, hereafter referred to as the project area.

The most fundamental assumption underlying this assessment is that sites within the project area represent a segment of wider regional settlement and subsistence systems operating on several levels. These systems certainly operate within the Sells Wash drainage, the Papaguería, and between the Papaguería and adjacent regions; undoubtedly, other levels of interaction also could be identified. It is further assumed that an understanding of these regional relationships is vital to an accurate assessment of cultural resources within the project area. Consequently, research undertaken for this assessment extended beyond the project boundaries. Chapter 2 describes the research methods. Chapter 3, the environmental setting of the Papaguería, Chapter 4, culture history, and Chapter 5, provide the interpretive framework for assessing sites in the project area. Chapters 6 and 7 focus more specifically on the project area and form the core of this report for planning purposes. Chapter 6 summarizes known cultural resources in the project area, identifies archaeologically sensitive areas and assesses the significance of the project area as a whole. Chapter 7 summarizes the impact of various existing natural and human disturbances and the probable effects of developments on the archaeological record of the project area. Specific recommendations for intensive survey and monitoring within the project area also are developed in Chapter 7; this assessment concludes with a summary statement of the findings of the report. References and Appendices follow the text.

This assessment, in sum, is addressed to two overlapping audiences--archaeologists and planners. Readers with management interests or requirements in the project area will find Chapters 6 and 7, and the appendices useful for their purposes. Those who wish a more detailed understanding of the basis of the findings in the management chapters or who have research interests in the Papaguería should consult Chapters 3 through 6.

CHAPTER 2

ASSESSMENT METHODS

Definition of Project Area

The primary focus of this report is a parcel of approximately 12.75 square miles in and around Sells, Arizona. Sells is about 60 miles southwest of Tucson, Arizona, in the southeastern quadrant of the 2 million-acre Papago Indian Reservation, established in 1918 between Tucson and Ajo, and between Chuichu and the International Boundary. A map provided by STRAAM Engineers, Inc., shows that this parcel includes all or portions of the following sections: Township 17 South, Range 4 East, Sections 15, 16, 21, 22, 23, 24, 25, 26, 35, and 36; and Township 17 South, Range 5 East, Sections 20, 29, 30, 31, and 32.

An additional area of approximately 3.5 square miles, comprising an extension to the well fields west of Sells and including part of the road between Sells and Gu Oidak (PIR 24), was shown on the map provided by STRAAM Engineers, Inc. This extension includes all or portions of the following sections: Township 17 South, Range 4 East, Sections 25 and 26; and Township 17 South, Range 4 East, Sections 27, 28, 29, 30, 31, 32, 33, and 34. Since the proposed modifications of sewer facilities do not extend into this parcel, it has not been incorporated in the project area; however, the general findings on known cultural resources and recommendations also are applicable to it. Surveyed areas and specific site data within this extension are on file at the Cultural Resource Management Section of the Arizona State Museum (ASM); the original site survey forms are housed at the Western Archeological Center (WAC) in Tucson and can be obtained from these institutions if future land modifications are undertaken in the extension.

The 12.75 square mile parcel is shown in Figures 1 and 2. The irregular boundaries of the project are arbitrary; however, the project area can be more conveniently described as a zone bounded by the main body of the Artesa Mountains on the south, Etoi Ki (an isolated hill) on the northwest, and the base of the upper bajada of the South Comobabi Mountains on the northeast.

This project area contains four prominent topographic features: (1) the northern extension of the Artesa Mountains, (2) isolated igenous formations (such as Etoi Ki) rising above the flood plain, (3) the flood plain or valley floor alluvial deposits, and (4) the Sells Wash, which flows through the project area.

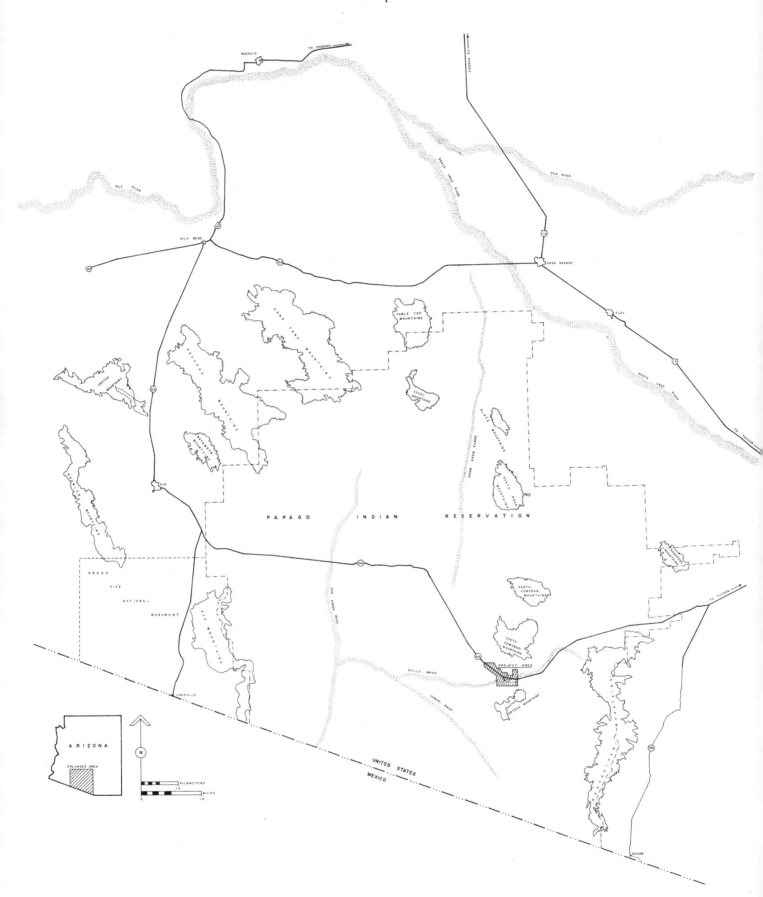

Figure 1. Sells Assessment Project Area in the central Papagueria

Summary of Research Methods

In order to provide planning information, a records check for previously recorded sites in the project area was undertaken. In addition to examining site files and Gila Pueblo records housed at the Arizona State Museum, the Cultural Resource Management Section of the Arizona State Museum requested site information for the project area from the following institutions: the San Diego Museum of Man, San Diego, California; Arizona Western College, Yuma, Arizona; Arizona State University, Tempe, Arizona; the Amerind Foundation, Dragoon, Arizona; the Museum of Northern Arizona, Flagstaff, and the Western Archeological Center, National Park Service, Tucson. Of these institutions, only the Arizona State Museum and Western Archeological Center have recorded sites in the project area. A check of the cultural resource records at the Arizona State Parks office in Phoenix, Arizona revealed that there were no cultural resource properties listed on the National or State Registers of Historic Places or the State Inventory.

A sketch of relevant characteristics of the general environment in which the project area is set was based on published summaries. Detailed data collection on vegetation communities, soils, and hydrology within the project area was beyond the scope of this assessment.

Once the records check and environmental sketch were completed, relevant published and unpublished archaeological research in and adjacent to the central Papaguería was reviewed. This was designed (1) to provide an interpretive framework for assessing the significance of sites within the project area, (2) to identify gaps or problems in the prehistory of the Papaguería that might be resolved by sites in the project area, and (3) to better predict where unrecorded sites in the project area might be discovered.

Existing disturbances within the project area were based on previous observations by archaeologists, on a consideration of topographic features, on a single visit to the project area, and on a study of Sells Wash and Little Tucson Wash by the U.S. Army Corps of Engineers (1976). Projected disturbances were based on the above factors, in conjunction with descriptions of proposed modifications in the sewer facilities in a draft report by STRAAM Engineers, Inc. (1978).

Finally, project area recommendations were developed. Specific recommendations for the proposed sewer facility modifications are first provided. Second, a complete inventory survey of the cultural resources in the project area is suggested as an effective long term planning tool. Specific and general recommendations are based on consideration of the nature of project area resources, their research potential, the archaeological sensitivity of the project area, and the nature of ground disturbance associated with planned development.

It should be emphasized that this report serves only as a preliminary statement about known and expected resources in the project area; it can be used as a starting point for future archaeological research and to identify for planners the archaeological factors that should be considered in development plans for Sells. This document is not intended, in any way, to represent a final statement on archaeological resources within the project area. No survey was undertaken for this assessment and survey coverage is incomplete in the project area. It is expected that many of the archaeological interpretations offered here will be substantially revised as research in the Papaguería progresses.

CHAPTER 3

ENVIRONMENTAL SETTING

This chapter provides a brief sketch of the environment of the Papaguería with a focus on what Hackenberg (1964) calls the central zone (defined below). This section is intended to provide information on the important characteristics of topography, hydrology, rainfall, and biotic communities in the Papaguería, since these are considered to be among the most important characteristics that conditioned human existence on the Papaguería during both the prehistoric and historic periods. It is expected that the distribution and density of archaeological sites on the landscape reflects, to a large degree, the availability of crucial local resources, given that prehistoric and historic Indian groups were dependent almost exclusively upon local resources for food, clothing, shelter, and tools. An understanding of environmental conditions, then, is crucial to reconstructing past lifeways. Such characteristics as elevation, soil substrate, availability of water and arable land, slope, exposure, topographic setting, biotic community, and proximity to adjacent environmental settings are all basic to an understanding of the inter-action between humans and their environment.

While a detailed analysis of the environmental features of the project area ideally should accompany any analysis of the project area's cultural resources, this chapter will offer only a more general des-cription of the central Papaguería as a whole, based on Hackenberg (1964), Stacy (1974) and McClellan and Vogler (1977). This approach has been selected for three reasons. First, the data indicate that during the course of a year historic period Papagos ranged over a fairly extensive area to practice ak chin cultivation and to gather needed resources; it is assumed that a large range of territory also was ex-ploited during Archaic and ceramic period times. It is likely, there-fore, that the inhabitants of the project area made use of resources outside the project area. Resources available outside the project area also must be considered in any discussion of the environmental context of cultural resources within the project area. Second, precise corre-lations between sites within the project area and environmental features cannot be made at this point because archaeological survey coverage within project boundaries is incomplete. Third, time constraints for this study precluded any analysis of the precise vegetation, soil, and hydro-logical data now available for the project area on Arid Lands studies maps. It is expected that future archaeological research within project boundaries will be accompanied by a fuller treatment of environmental data specific to the project area.

The Papaguería: Western, Central and Eastern Zones

The Papaguería is defined as the region bounded on the east by the Santa Cruz River, on the north by the Gila River Valley, on the west by the Colorado River and on the south by the International Boundary (Hackenberg 1964: 11-21). The latter is an arbitrary boundary, since Papago territory extended southward into Sonora, Mexico; it will be used in this report, however, since more data are available for the area north of the International Boundary. Hackenberg subdivides the Papaguería into three "life zones," each possessing characteristic biotic and cultural features. These are: the western zone from the Colorado River to the Growler Mountains, the central zone from the Growler Mountains to the Baboquivari Mountains, and the eastern zone from the Baboquivari Mountains to the Santa Cruz River. The western zone which falls within the Lower Colorado Valley division of the Lower Sonoran Life Zone, is characterized by extreme aridity and was sparsely populated in historic times by the Sand Papago, a group of nomadic hunters and gatherers. The central zone falls within the Arizona Upland division of the Lower Sonoran Life Zone; it is characterized by higher rainfall and, in historic times, by more people residing in field and well villages on a semi-annual basis. The eastern zone is sharply demarcated from the central zone by the transition from desert flora west of the Baboquivari Mountains to grassland vegetation east of the mountains. The Upper Sonoran Life Zone vegetation characteristic of the eastern zone reflects higher rainfall there than in the central zone. The eastern zone was more densely populated, with historic Papago groups living in permanent, irrigation-based villages. Since the project area lies at the eastern periphery of the central zone, discussion here will focus on the central zone and relevant aspects of the eastern zone.

The lowland (alluvial valley floor) regions of the central zone include the Ajo valley; the southeast extensions of Sentinel Plain and Gila Bend Plain (along Sauceda Wash); the Rainbow, Vekol and San Simon valleys; the Santa Rosa, Gu Oidak and Tecolote valleys, and the Baboquivari and Aguirre valleys. Within the central zone, less than half of the intermontane area is composed of level plains, or bajadas, on a low gradient (under two degrees); the remainder consists of steeper upper bajadas (two to four degrees gradient). The alluvial deposits found in the valleys vary in depth, but soils generally become finer grained and deeper as one moves toward the center of the valley.

The valleys in the central zone are separated by mountain ranges composed of a mixture of volcanic and sedimentary rocks. From west to east these are the Little Ajo Mountains; a mountain chain composed of the Sauceda, Batamote, Pozo Redondo and Great Ajo mountains; the Sand Tank Mountains, a southern extension, and the Mesquite Mountains; Table Top Mountains; the Vekol and Quijotoa mountains, and the Tat Momoli; Santa Rosa, Comobabi and Artesa mountains. The elevations of the valley floors and mountains rise on a gradient from west to east. In the northern portion, valleys decrease in elevation as they approach the Gila River Valley.

The central zone exhibits several characteristics resulting from greater precipitation than is found further west. Among these features are:

1. less steep mountain slopes and wider pediments;
2. sloping, rather than flat, valley floors;
3. alluvial fan formation at the mouths of washes, suitable for ak chin farming; and,
4. heavier soil deposition on bajadas below the mountains.

Precipitation tends to increase on a gradient from west to east within the Papaguería, as does the tendency toward summer-dominant rainfall. In the central zone, the biseasonal distribution of rainfall results in wetter conditions between July and August and from December through March. Of the two intervening dry seasons, the fall is less severe. In summer, storms occur as short, sporadic, intense afternoon and evening thunderstorms originating in the Gulf of Mexico. These high energy systems generally result in heavier localized runoff and greater channel and sheet wash flooding than do winter storms. The latter are typically large scale cyclonic Pacific Ocean storms characterized by steady light rains one or more days in duration. Annual precipitation gradients average 5-inches, 10-inches, and 15-inches as defined by Hackenberg (1964: 11-8). The 5-inch gradient is a southwesterly line running 25 miles west of Ajo. The 10-inch gradient runs from Sonoita, Mexico, northeasterly through Casa Grande. The 15-inch line runs north-south along the Santa Cruz Valley. The project area lies within the region receiving an annual average of 10 to 15 inches of rainfall, although the Corps of Engineers cites a somewhat higher figure (15 to 20 inches) (U.S. Army Corps of Engineers 1976: 3).

Within the Papaguería higher amounts of rainfall (11 to 20 inches) are distributed in mountain ranges, with both the highest elevation (7730 feet) and highest average annual rainfall (19.91 inches) found in the Baboquivari Mountains east of Sells (Hackenberg 1964: 11-4).

Temperatures across the Papaguería vary within a more limited range. Hackenberg (1964: 11-4) provides comparative data on mean maxima and minima for the hottest and coldest months (July and January) in Tucson, Sells, Ajo and Yuma. These show that the maximum difference in mean temperatures among the four towns is consistently less than ten degrees Fahrenheit. While there is more variation in the number of frost-free days, the effective growing season throughout the Papaguería is fairly uniform, when the amount and distribution of rainfall is taken into consideration (Hackenberg 1964: 11-5).

The Central Zone: Hydrology and Biotic Communities

Hydrology

Drainage systems in the central zone flow directly toward the Gila River, indirectly toward the Gila River via the Santa Rosa Wash system, or into the Sonoita River (Mexico) via the south-trending San Simon Wash. The project area, drained by Sells Wash, is in the latter system.

An arc of amorphous mountain chains forms the divide between the Santa Rosa Valley, the San Simon Valley and the drainages that flow into the Gila River. This arc, which opens to the south, consists of (in clockwise direction from west to east): the Ajo, Sikort Chuapo, Sauceda and Sand Tank mountains; an unnamed range containing Cimarron's Peak, and the Quijotoa, South Comobabi and Baboquivari mountains. To the west and north of this arc drainages flow northwest into the Gila River. On the north and east, drainages flow toward Santa Rosa Basin.

The Santa Rosa drainage is a north-trending system originating at Quijotoa and passing between the Tat Momoli, Slate and Santa Rosa mountains on the east and the Quijotoa, Cimarron, Sheridan, Vekol, and Table Top mountains on the west. The Santa Rosa Wash flows into the Gila River north of the Papago Indian Reservation. Ephemeral north-trending streams also drain the Aguirre Valley east of the Santa Rosa Basin.

The San Simon drainage basin, which ultimately flows southward into the Sonoita River, drains the south side of the above mentioned arc of mountains. The Vamori Wash and its tributaries (the Sells, Fresnal, Baboquivari and Chutum Vaya washes) form a major component of the San Simon drainage system. These ephemeral streams descend in a westerly and northwesterly direction from the Baboquivari Mountains across the Baboquivari Valley and join the San Simon Wash near the modern village of Kom Vo. With the exception of two small streams in the Baboquivari Mountains, no permanent water courses are found in the central zone; all valleys are drained by ephemeral, intermittently flowing washes. Despite the lack of permanent streams, suitable locations for wells exist in the Papaguería. The foothills of such ranges as the Baboquivari, Comobabi and Quijotoa mountains comprise one such location in the central zone. There, crystalline rock formations raise the water table closer to the ground surface, where it was tapped by hand-dug Papago wells during the 19th century (Hackenberg 1964: IV-65). Papagos also used water that collected in natural rock basins (tinajas or tanks) in the mountains. On the valley floor water flowed along natural channels into shallow, natural or man-made depressions (charcos or reservoirs). Both tinajas and charcos are subject to high evaporation rates and are, therefore, impermanent supplies (Hackenberg 1964: II-9).

Biotic Communities

   Vegetation. The central zone lies within a region classified as
a Crassicaulescent (stem-succulent) desert. This region is characterized
by a predominance of Cercidium (palo-verde) and Opuntia (prickly-pear and
cholla cacti). The vegetation in this region exceeds that of the western
zone in density, variety, and size. Larrea (creosote-bush) is abundant,
but is associated with a wider variety of plants than in the western zone.
Vegetation is differentially distributed on several topographic features
characteristic of the Arizona Upland. Based on data from Shreve and
Wiggins (1964: 60-80), Stacy (1974: 51-3, 72) defined the characteristics
of these topographic features, washes and streamways, plains and lower
bajadas, upper bajadas, and hills and mountain slopes (all of which occur
in the Baboquivari Valley). These features are discussed below.

   The moister conditions of washes and streamways support larger,
denser concentrations of plants common in other areas, as well as
species not found elsewhere. Mesic species, such as Quercus (oak),
border the rocky streambeds near the mountain sources of the washes.
Desert (Xeric) plants, such as Populus (cottonwood), Salix (willow),
Juglans (walnut) and Prosopis (mesquite), also grow in this setting.
Alluvial flood plains, where fine-grained deposits are carried by slow
moving water, formerly supported dense stands of Prosopis, but because of
extensive cutting and farming these occur today as more open stands.
Sandy flood plains subject to flash flooding are dominated by shrubby
species, such as Baccharis sarothroides (desert-broom) and Hymenoclea
monogyra (burro-bush).

   The sandy loam soils of the plains and lower bajadas of the level
valley floor support Larrea (creosote-bush), Acacia constricta (white-thorn
acacia), A. Greggii (catclaw acacia) and Prosopis juliflora var. velutena
(mesquite), as well as several species of Opuntia. Field observations
by Stacy indicated that the valley floor in the vicinity of the Comobabi,
Artesa and Quinlan mountains is dominated by creosote-bush or mesquite,
followed by bur-sage and cholla or prickly-pear species.

   Upper bajadas support a number of perennials of economic importance
to historic Papagos. These include Larrea, Cercidium microphyllum, Opuntia,
Fouquieria splendens (ocotillo), Lycium andersonii (wolf-berry), Condalia
lycioides (gray-thorn), Celtis pallida (hackberry) and Prosopis juliflora
var. velutina. Franseria deltoidea (bur-sage) and Encelia farinosa (brittle-
bush) also are found in this setting. The bajadas in the Quinlan, Comobabi,
and Artesa mountains were dominated by palo-verde or cholla, with brittle-
bush being the most common subdominant species.

   Hills and mountain slopes support a similar assemblage; spacing
between plants reflects localized features, such as soil depth, moisture
and exposure. The Baboquivari Mountains, classified as part of the more
mesic eastern zone, support palo-verde on the lower slopes, desert grass

at a slightly higher elevation and oak-chapparal species and agave on their upper slopes.

The Baboquivari Valley, located in the eastern periphery of the central zone, is within range of the unique resources of the Baboquivari Mountains, which along with the Comobabi and Quijotoa mountains constituted the richer collecting areas in the central zone. Hackenberg (1964: II, 38-50) provides a list of uses to which over 65 kinds of wild plants were put by the Papagos. Stacy (1974: 59-69) also compiled extensive tables summarizing the distribution of plants collected during the Papago seasonal rounds. These two references should be consulted for the detailed subsistence data they provide. Table 1 below, extracted from a summary of the most important economic species, indicates the general locations and seasons for collecting several economic plants.

Table 1. Distribution and Collection Period of Plant
Species of Economic Importance to Historic Papago

Species	Location	Collection Period
Pig-weed (Amaranthus)	valley floor	between July and November
Goose-foot (Chenopodium)	valley floor	between July and November
Hackberry (Celtis)	valley floor	between July and November
Bur-sage (Franseria)	valley floor	between July and November
Mesquite (Prosopis)	valley floor	between July and November
Canaigre (Rumex)	valley floor	March, April
Prickly-pear, cholla (Opuntia spp.)	bajada	between July and November, spring
Palo-verde (Cercidium)	bajada	between July and November
Saguaro (Carnegiea)	bajada	between July and November
Datil (Yucca)	bajada	between July and November
Wild potato (Solanum)	mountain slopes	summer
Oak (Quercus)	mountain slopes	summer
Chillipiquin (Capsicum)	mountain slopes	summer
Agave	mountain slopes	winter
Sotol (Dasyliron)	mountain slopes	winter
Papago blue-bells (Dichelostemma)	mountain slopes	winter
Wild onion (Allium)	mountain slopes	winter

Animals. A variety of animal species commonly are found in the Arizona Upland region (Hackenberg 1964: IV-77), but their distributions more closely reflect terrain and the availability of water than plant distribution per se (McClellan and Vogler 1977: 21). In addition to coyote, fox, bobcat, javelina, antelope, bighorn sheep, desert cottontail, white-tailed deer and desert tortoise, which are found throughout the Papaguería (Hackenberg 1964: II-22), a number of species occur only in the central zone. Hackenberg (1964: IV-77) identifies these as:

Black-tailed jack rabbit (Lepus californicus deserticola)
Harris' antelope squirrel (Citellus harrisii saxicola)
Round-tailed ground squirrel (Citellus tereticaudus)
Arizona pocket mouse (Perognathus amplus rotundus)
Bailey's pocket mouse (Perognathus baileyi domensis)
Desert kangaroo rat (Dipodomys deserti deserti)
White-throated wood rat (Neotoma albigula venusta)
White-throated wood rat (Neotoma albigula mearnsi)
Desert wood rat (Neotoma lepida flava)
Desert wood rat (Neotoma lepida auripila)
Desert wood rat (Neotoma lepida bensoni)
Mountain lion (Felis concolor browni)
Mule deer (Odocoileus hemionus eremicus)

The Arizona Upland is a game-rich area. Mule deer and several varieties of rabbits reach their greatest abundance within the south-eastern portion of the central zone (Hackenberg 1964: IV, 77-8).

Conclusion

In reviewing the environmental characteristics of the central zone, it is important to note that the project area lies within one of the more abundant locales within the central zone and is adjacent to the Baboquivari Mountains, where unique plant and animal species are found. Located at the interface between the central and eastern zones, the valley west of the Baboquivari Mountains and immediately east of Sells receives greater summer and winter rainfall than do areas further west. As a result, species scarce or absent elsewhere in the central zone of the Papaguería occur in greater abundance in the eastern periphery. The greater variety and densities of plant and animal species characteristic of the valleys and bajadas immediately west of the Baboquivari Mountains indicate that a greater human population density could be supported in this area than elsewhere in the central zone during historic times. Assuming that major environmental changes have not taken place since prehistoric times, this pattern presumably existed in earlier periods as well.

Past Environments: The Papaguería

The question of whether the present environment resembles past conditions remains a debated issue. Within the past 100 years alone, widespread arroyo cutting, grassland deterioration and invasion of grasslands by woody species throughout southern Arizona have altered the productivity of the land; similar cycles of erosion are also known to have occurred prehistorically. An amalgam of conditions, including changing rainfall patterns, cattle grazing, road cutting, suppression of fires and increased rodent population, have been identified as probable factors in the onset of the most recent erosional cycles. The causes of earlier erosion episodes are unclear.

Despite the presence of erosional cycles, there appears to be long term stability of overall environmental conditions in the Papaguería. From at least the prehistoric ceramic period to the present (roughly the last 1,200 years) there is little evidence of major displacement of vegetation communities within the Papaguería. Consequently, it seems safe to assume that Desert Hohokam period and present plant and animal species are comparable in density and distribution.

The question of environmental change for the earlier prehistoric periods remains controversial. McClellan and Vogler (1977: 7-9) summarize the problems of reconstructing past environments; their discussion is excerpted, in part, below.

Reconstructing the prehistoric environment is difficult. Not only are the causes of fluctuations, if there were any, unclear, but the actual state of the past environment is hotly disputed. One approach used geologic processes, fossils, radiocarbon dates and tree rings, from which past climatic conditions were inferred (Antevs 1955). The resulting Bryan-Antevs model postulated a wet, cool pluvial period at about 11,000 years ago, followed by a warmer, drier post pluvial period, which was divided as follows:

Medithermal 4,000 B.P. - Present
Altithermal 7,500 B.P. - 4,000 B.P.
Anathermal 10,000 B.P. - 7,500 B.P.

The Altithermal period was interpreted as having much hotter and drier drought conditions than are evident today, with the Medithermal exhibiting a number of relatively short periods of drought. Using the Bryan-Antevs model, archaeological remains associated with extinct mammals were assigned to the pluvial period. Denser vegetation was assumed necessary to sustain these large mammals and increasing dessication was considered the cause of their extinction (Antevs 1959: 32).

More recently, faunal and floral remains in glacial and post-glacial packrat middens from deserts of the southwestern United States have been radiocarbon dated and analyzed (Van Devender 1973). During the late Pleistocene, woodland and chaparral communities descended into desert regions, with single-needle pinyon found as low as 510 m (ca. 1675 feet) and more xeric, juniper woodland as low as 320 m (ca. 1050 feet). Many desert species were associated with the woodland plants (Van Devender 1973). Several plants that now are dominant in the Mohave Desert to the north but are not presently found in the Sonoran Desert were located as far south as the Ajo Mountains in Organ Pipe National Monument (Van Devender 1977). Van Devender concluded that the development (or northward movement from Mexico) of desertscrub and grassland communities and the drying of playa lakes occurred about 8,000 years ago as the direct result of a decrease in winter precipitation. This shift in climate was the result of the recession of glaciers, which took thousands of years to complete. Van Devender's evidence suggests that a transitional xeric woodland may have existed between 11,000 and 8,000 years ago. According to Van Devender (1977), the transition to desert climates and vegetation came after the extinction of many large mammals, suggesting that factors other than changes in climate and vegetation were responsible for their extinction. In contrast to the extinction of large mammals, the late Pleistocene reptile, amphibian and small mammal populations were similar to modern faunas (Van Devender 1973). Van Devender (1977) associated Paleo-Indian cultures with late Pleistocene mesic woodland settings, thus correlating cultural transitions with subsequent changes in climate and vegetation.

Although microenvironmental changes most certainly have occurred, most evidence now points to overall stability since the end of glacial conditions. As the present environment is all that is available for the archaeological surveyor to record, care should be taken to note as many different factors that might conceivably affect a site's microenvironmental setting as possible, in the hope that constraints in change and stability will be discovered. Researchers should be aware of the research potential of sites with cultural depth from which pollen and macrofossil samples can be analyzed, and check rock shelters and caves for the presence of packrat middens.

As can be seen from the above discussion, reconstruction of the prehistoric environment is presently in a state of controversy. As knowledge of the past environment is necessary for an understanding of prehistoric cultures, further geological, palynological and macrofossil studies are vital.

Summary

In this chapter the topographic, hydrological and rainfall regimes that influence the three biotic zones defined by Hackenberg for the Papaguería have been examined. The project area has been shown to occupy an interface between the central zone and the less arid eastern zone. This region has been characterized as a rich gathering area, exhibiting a relatively dense distribution of a wide range of plant and animal species. Additional varieties of plants and animals are found in close proximity in the Baboquivari Mountains. Water can be tapped with hand-dug wells in areas near the base of the Baboquivari Mountains because of a suitable geological substrate.

The following two chapters (a culture history of the Papaguería and adjacent regions and a history of archaeological research in the central zone) discuss our knowledge of past human adaptations to the environment outlined in this chapter.

CHAPTER 4

CULTURE HISTORY

On the most basic level of understanding, archaeological remains are interpreted within the framework of a regional culture history. The development of such a framework for the central Papaguería has been hampered by a lack of systematic regional investigations, and by conflicting interpretations of the archaeological data gathered to date. The framework provided here for the preceramic period has been excerpted, with minor changes, from McClellan and Vogler (1977), who dealt with past research in southwestern Arizona in their assessment of the Luke Air Force Range west of the Papago Indian Reservation. Discussion of the prehistoric (ceramic) period is drawn from McClellan and Vogler (1977) and from Debowski and others (1976), who discussed remains from the Salt-Gila Basin. The historic summary is based on Hackenberg (1964), Fontana (1964), Clotts (1915) and Stacy (1974). This regional perspective provides the framework within which resources in the project area can be interpreted and their significance assessed.

Early Man

An Early Man hunting complex originally was described for the Nevada and California deserts and later identified in western and southern Arizona and northwestern Sonora. The terms Malpais, San Dieguito, and Ventana complex have been used to describe this early culture.

Working in deserts adjacent to the Colorado River, Rogers (1939: 6-22) originally defined a Malpais industry. He used this term to separate materials from a later industry he then called the San Dieguito-Playa complex. Rogers later re-evaluated the evidence and combined the Malpais and San Dieguito-Playa industries into the San Dieguito complex. The Malpais industry became Phase I of the San Dieguito complex (Rogers 1958: 3).

Rogers did not have the advantage of sites with vertical depth. He used a horizontal stratigraphy technique that correlated artifacts with physiographic features. Those materials associated with ancient landforms were considered the oldest. At that time Rogers (1958: 20) assigned a conservative beginning date of 2000 B.C. for the San Dieguito complex.

The San Dieguito I materials consisted of sparsely scattered, crude percussion flaked artifacts made from local gravels and cobbles. The high degree of patination and oxidation on the artifacts helped determine their relative antiquity. The scattered nature of the

artifacts reflected a highly unsettled living pattern. Chopper
tools often were discarded at the place they were manufactured and used.
This reflected the abundant availability of raw lithic material and
the ease with which these crude tools could be made. The lack of
stone projectile points in this hunting industry suggests the presence
of wood or bone points. Because the materials were on the surface, there
were no associated faunal remains. In addition to the flake and core
tools, other features of this industry included circular or oval sleeping
clearings and geometric figures (intaglio figures) arranged from gravel
(Rogers 1939: 6-22).

The Ventana complex, a term used to identify the lowest culture
level at Ventana Cave in southern Arizona was basically a San Dieguito
I assemblage (Haury 1950: 193; Rogers 1958: 4). Rogers (1958) also
identified San Dieguito materials along the Rincon-Pantano and Rillito
drainage system east and southeast of Tucson. He compared San Dieguito
I artifacts found in the Nevada and California deserts with those found
in Arizona at Ventana Cave and along the Pantano drainage system. The
Arizona pattern was somewhat more developed than either the Nevada or
California pattern. This difference probably resulted from the time factor
involving the spread of the complex into Arizona (Rogers 1958: 15-16).

The assignment of a new term, the Ventana complex, resulted from
problems in correlating the age of the Ventana Cave assemblage with
Rogers' dates. Ventana Cave had the advantage of vertical stratigraphy
and confirmed the relative placement of the San Dieguito complex below
the later desert hunting industry. Geologic interpretation of the strata,
association of extinct fauna, and radiocarbon dates placed the Ventana
complex at 10,000 years ago (Haury 1950; Haury's 1975 preface of the
reprint of Ventana Cave). Rogers (1966: 140) later revised his dates
to reflect greater antiquity for the San Dieguito complex.

Hayden recently has revived the idea of a basal Malpais phase,
which he believes evolved into San Dieguito I. Hayden's (1976) description
of this early man hunting complex is based on his work in the Sierra
Pinacates in Sonora.

A major distinguishing factor between the cultural remains of
the two phases is varnish. The earlier Malpais tools have a heavier
varnish than do the later San Dieguito I tools. The Malpais phase
occupants used local "tabular basalt blocks or basaltic pyroclastic ejecta"
to make tools. The later San Dieguito I people made tools from larger
quarry blocks, a process requiring more reduction flaking. All tools
of both phases were percussion flaked and indicated woodworking activities. Malpais tools included knives, spokeshaves, hollow-sided scrapers,
notched and beaked tools, and choppers. Shell from the Gulf of California
was also percussion flaked and used as small knives, scrapers and gouges.
These shell tools are distinguishable from later ones by their gray color.
Some of the San Dieguito tools were bifacially flaked and included unifacial choppers and scrapers, Levallois-like flake tools, tabular cores
for making blades and flakes, smaller and more varied scrapers,

perforators, spokeshaves, and notched and beaked tools (Hayden 1976: 281-84). There also is evidence for the possible beginnings of ground stone in the San Dieguito I phase (Haury 1950: 187-88; Hayden 1976: 285). Other features of this early complex include trails, stone shrines and cairns, intaglio figures, and sleeping circles. During the San Dieguito I phase the intaglio figures became less complex and the sleeping circles were stone-lined (Hayden 1976: 285).

There is evidence for relatively moist conditions during San Dieguito I times. Rogers (1939: 21) originally defined the San Dieguito complex by its association with ancient landforms where sources of water no longer exist. Extinct fauna found with the Ventana complex point to moister conditions and better foraging (Haury 1950: 137, 191-93).

So far the basal Malpais phase has been identified only in the Sierra Pinacates (Hayden 1976). San Dieguito I materials have been identified in Nevada, California, Baja California, northwestern Sonora, and western and southern Arizona (Haury 1950; Hayden 1976; Rogers 1939, 1958, 1966). There is no evidence for San Dieguito II or III in southern Arizona or Sonora (Hayden 1976; Rogers 1958: 21).

The Sulphur Spring stage of the Cochise culture was the earliest phase of another subsistence pattern that developed in southeastern Arizona. Although the Sulphur Spring stage was associated with extinct fauna, it represented primarily a ground stone industry, with vegetal food gathering dominant over hunting (Sayles and Antevs 1941: 14). Rogers (1958: 10) noted a similarity between the chipped stone patterns of the Sulphur Spring stage and the San Dieguito I complex. The San Dieguito complex originally was interpreted as a hunting industry, although recent work has indicated that food gathering also played some part in the subsistence pattern (King 1977). The differences between the two cultures probably represent adaptations to different environments (Hayden 1970: 88). Whether the two patterns date from the same period is not known. The Sulphur Spring assemblage is not present at Ventana Cave (Haury 1950: 319) or elsewhere in the Papaguería.

Archaic

Following the San Dieguito I occupation, southwestern Arizona and northwestern Sonora apparently were abandoned. Although conflicting opinions exist, the abandonment may have been brought on by a period of extremely arid climatic conditions. This dry period may have lasted as long as 5,000 years (Haury 1950: 522; Hayden 1976: 285). During this time many sources of water dried up and many animals not adapted to dry climate became extinct.

With the return of somewhat moister conditions (Hayden 1976: 285), a new stock of people, who originated in the Great Basin vicinity

(Hayden 1970: 88), migrated into southern Arizona and northern
Mexico. These Amargosan people occupied the same area and probably
more than that previously used by the San Dieguitoans (Rogers 1958: 6,
17). Hayden's (1967: 337) "clear cut and prolonged hiatus between
San Dieguito phase I and Amargosa phase I" coincides with a
gap in cultural materials between the Ventana complex and Amargosan materials at Ventana Cave (Haury 1950: 295). In Arizona there is a direct
relationship between Amargosan sites and modern sources of water
(Rogers 1958: 6, 17) and an association with modern fauna (Haury 1950: 538).

The original description of the Amargosa I and II complexes
combined previous work done at Pinto Basin in California and Gypsum
Cave in Nevada. The most common tools associated with this hunting
complex were pulping planes, various kinds of hand-held choppers, and
projectile points, including five Pinto point types and the Gypsum
Cave point. Less abundant were hammerstones, scrapers, knives,
bone tools, and possibly borers and reamers (Rogers 1939: 47-60). Differences between the Amargosa complex in Nevada and California and
in the Papaguería are related to the latter area's contact with the
Cochise culture, as evidenced by the presence of southeastern Arizona
point types and the appearance of metates during Amargosa II times (Rogers
1958: 6).

In the Pinacate region the Amargosa artifacts lack desert
varnish, although some are lightly oxidized. Amargosa rock features
still have caliche deposits encrusted on them. The caliche on features
made by the earlier Malpais and San Dieguito people has mostly dis-
solved (Hayden 1976: 277, 280). Features assigned to the Amargosa I
phase include the continued use of the same network of trails used by
the San Dieguitoans, camp clearings or sleeping clearings (larger than
the earlier sleeping circles), linear or curvilinear lava cobble-
lined figures on the desert pavement, and stone shrines. The Amargosa
phase II artifacts exhibit less patination than do Amargosa I tools.
Amargosa II is further distinguished by new point types and the addition
of the metate. The above listed features continue during the second phase,
with the addition of stone windbreaks open to one side. The earlier stone-
lined San Dieguito I sleeping circles were fully enclosed (Hayden 1967:
337, 339).

Elements of the Chiricahua and San Pedro stages of the Cochise
culture in southeastern Arizona have been found associated with the
Amargosa complex in the Papaguería. The Chiricahua stage is inter-
mediate between the earlier Sulphur Spring and later San Pedro stages.
During the Chiricahua times ground stone continued to be the dominant
tool type. Most of the chipped stone tools still were percussion
flaked. The few pressure flaked points were considered intrusive.
This Chiricahua stage tool kit indicates a continued heavy dependence
on gathered vegetal foods, although hunting was part of the subsistence
pattern. During the San Pedro stage chipped tools were more numerous for

the first time than ground stone tools. The increase in pressure flaking, particularly of projectile points, indicated the increased importance of hunting (Sayles and Antevs 1941: 19-28).

At Ventana Cave, Amargosa I and II materials were in evidence. Influence from southeastern Arizona was apparent during Amargosa II times, culminating in a dominance of San Pedro elements. The Papaguería lacked the well developed sequences of ground stone found with the Cochise culture. At Ventana Cave, Chiricahua style milling stones persisted into later times. It was the diagnostic projectile points, particularly the San Pedro points, that most clearly indicated increased contact with southeastern Arizona (Haury 1950: 319, 531-34).

The Papaguería Amargosan I and II phases basically formed a hunting complex (Rogers 1958: 4). Possibly due to increased contact with southeastern Arizona, gathered vegetal foods acquired increased importance through time. Although generally considered a preceramic assemblage, some Amargosa II tools have been found associated with early ceramics (Hayden 1967: 339; Hayden 1970: 89; Rogers 1958: 21). This may represent contemporaneity or transition for Amargosan II and ceramic cultures.

Before giving a summary of the ceramic period groups, a few comments on the possible linkage between Amargosan preceramic people and ceramic groups are in order. According to Hayden, the Amargosans who migrated to the Pinacate region deviated from the general Amargosa culture pattern because of the region's unique environmental setting. He states that there is evidence for a continuous occupation of the Pinacates by Amargosans from Amargosa I into historic times. The historic occupants of the Pinacates were Pinacateños Areneños (Hayden 1967: 337-38). In his recording of Areneños remains, Fontana (1965: 93) also noted the continuation of an early subsistence pattern, with the addition primarily of ceramics. Both groups of Areneños spoke dialects of Papago, a Piman language. Hayden (1967: 343) extends this descent from the Amargosans to all Piman speakers whose cultural differences are explained as the result of adaptations to different environments.

At Ventana Cave, Haury (1950: 358) noted a similar continuation from the San Pedro to the Desert Hohokam culture, particularly in the survival of many of the lithic elements. There was no gap between the Amargosa I and II phases and the San Pedro materials (Haury 1950: 297-98).

Connecting prehistoric groups to historic groups is problematic, owing to our lack of knowledge of the protohistoric period. Haury (1950: 542) speculated on a Riverine Hohokam-Pima and Desert Hohokam-Papago continuum. By extension, this would give the Pimas and Papagos an Amargosan ancestry.

Gaps in our knowledge relevant to the transition of preceramic to ceramic and prehistoric to historic make the establishment of any direct lineal descent highly tentative. Evidence from recent surveys (Rosenthal and others 1978; Stacy 1975) suggests that further research may provide the means for determining such linkages.

Following is a summary of several prehistoric ceramic period and historic Indian groups that occupied an area bounded by the Santa Cruz, Gila and Colorado rivers on the east, north and west, and by the International Boundary on the south.

Hohokam

The following discussion of the Hohokam period (approximately 300 B.C. to A.D. 1450) is divided into sections on the "River Hohokam" and the "Desert Hohokam," following the formulation by Haury (1950). While some disagreement exists over the validity of this model (Hayden 1970; Ezell 1954; DiPeso 1956), it is used here to outline the variability in material culture and in adaptations to different environments within the Sonoran Desert. For both the River and Desert Hohokam, archaeologists have divided the cultural sequences into periods and subdivided these into phases. For the River Hohokam the broad changes characteristic of each period are discussed; because the River Hohokam are peripheral to the study area a detailed treatment of each phase is not deemed necessary. Discussion of the Desert Hohokam who occupied the project area is necessarily more detailed and is divided into phases. Table 2 illustrates the chronological relationships between the sequences for the River and Desert Hohokam.

Haury's concept of the River and Desert Hohokam, first outlined in the classic Ventana Cave report (Haury 1950), is an attempt to delineate and explain the differences and similarities between the material culture found along permanent water courses in the Gila-Salt Basin and in the harsher desert areas drained by impermanent streams. Haury's (1950: 547) trait comparison of the two areas, still a valid summary of the major differences in material culture after roughly A.D. 1000, is excerpted here:

River Branch	Desert Branch
Cremation	Earth burial
Red-on-buff pottery, not polished	Red-on-brown pottery, polished
Red ware, black interiors	Red ware, red interiors
Full troughed metate, well shaped	Block metate, some shaping, usually not troughed
Great array of projectile points, delicate workmanship	Limited projectile point types, few in number, workmanship inferior
Well developed carved stone	Carved stone weakly represented
Few chopping, scraping and cutting tools	Abundance of roughly chipped chopping, scraping and cutting tools
Slate palette	
Stone and shell jewelry abundant and elaborate	Slate palette, little used
Figurine complex strong	

River Branch	Desert Branch
Large-scale irrigation systems, drawing water from streams	Stone and shell jewelry, rare and simple
Subsistence primarily agriculture	Figurines, rare
Heavy Salado intrusion after 1300	Limited irrigation canals, designed to catch surface runoff
	Subsistence primarily collecting
	Little affected by Salado

According to Haury (1950: 46), the characteristics distinguishing the Papaguería from the Gila-Salt Basin appear toward the end of the Colonial period and become further elaborated until the end of the prehistoric Hohokam period. Based on geographical distribution of the traits listed above, the River Hohokam are defined as groups of related peoples who lived along the Gila, Salt and Santa Cruz rivers. In contrast, the Desert Hohokam occupied a region between Ajo and the Avra Valley on the west and east and between Chuichu and the International Boundary on the north and south. Haury (1950: 14) suggests that the relationship between the River and Desert Hohokam was analogous to that between the later Pimas and Papagos. Thus, although he acknowledges the affinities between the Papaguería and the Trincheras Complex to the south and the Tucson Basin to the east, he stresses the overall similarities between the Papaguería and the Gila-Salt Basin. The differences between the two areas are attributed to the different subsistence adaptations practiced in riverine and desert settings. In the Gila-Salt Basin, irrigation agriculture predominated over food-collecting, allowing larger, denser settlements and a greater elaboration of material culture, probably accompanied by a more complex formal social organization. In the harsher environment of the Papaguería, food collecting, supplemented by flood-water agriculture, was the dominant subsistence mode; settlements were smaller and more dispersed, and material culture and probably social organization were less elaborate. These basic differences are discussed in greater detail below.

River Hohokam

Before proceeding with a description of the River Hohokam cultural sequence, it is necessary to discuss the dating procedures used by researchers working on the Hohokam chronology. The Hohokam sequence is defined primarily on the basis of the excavations at Snaketown (Gladwin and others 1937; Haury 1976). Snaketown ceramics initially were cross-dated by correlation with intrusive sherds that had been dendrochronologically dated at northern Arizona sties. In turn, Hohokam sites outside the Salt-Gila Basin have been ceramically dated by comparison with the Snaketown materials. While theoretical problems with this method remain, it is important to note that the ceramically dated sequences from Snaketown have largely been verified by absolute dates obtained from radiocarbon and

| | DESERT HOHOKAM | RIVER HOHOKAM | | RIVER HOHOKAM | |
	PAPAGUERÍA[1]	TUCSON BASIN[2]	GILA BASIN[3]	GILA BASIN[4] 1976 (revised)	
A.D.1400	SELLS A.D.1250-1400 (CLASSIC)	TUCSON	CIVANO A.D.1300-1400	CIVANO A.D.1300-1450	CLASSIC
		TANQUE VERDE	SOHO 1200 or 1250-1300 (AD)	SOHO A.D.1100-1300	
1200	TOPAWA A.D.1100-1250 (SEDENTARY)	CORTARO ?	SANTAN A.D.1100-1200		
1000	VAMORI A.D.800-1100	RINCON	SACATON A.D.900-1100	SACATON A.D.900-1100	SEDENTARY
800	(COLONIAL)	RILLITO	SANTA CRUZ A.D.700-900	SANTA CRUZ A.D.700-900	COLONIAL
600		CAÑADA DEL ORO	GILA BUTTE A.D.500-700	GILA BUTTE A.D.550-700	
400	(PIONEER)	SNAKETOWN	SNAKETOWN A.D.300-500	SNAKETOWN A.D.350-550	PIONEER
200		SWEETWATER ? (isolated sherd)	SWEETWATER A.D.100-300	SWEETWATER A.D.200-350	
A.D.1			ESTRELLA 100B.C.-A.D.100	ESTRELLA A.D.100-200	
200 B.C.			VAHKI 300 B.C.- 100 B.C.	VAHKI 300 B.C.-A.D.1	

1. AFTER HAURY (1950: 6-13,16, Figure 2).
2. AFTER HAURY (1950:16, Figure 2); KELLY (1978: 4, Table 1.1).
3. AFTER HAURY (1950:16, Figure 2); KELLY (1978:4, Table 1.1).
4. AFTER HAURY (1976:338, Table 16.1). NOTE REVISED DATE FOR SEDENTARY/ CLASSIC TRANSITION.

Table 2. Chronological relationships between the River and Desert Hohokam sequences.

archaeomagnetic samples (Haury 1976). Therefore, Haury's (1976: 338, Table 16.1), suggested chronology, shown in the right hand column of Table 2, will be followed here.

Pioneer Period, 300 B.C. - A.D. 550.   The question of Hohokam origins remains unresolved. About 300 B.C. a new and fully developed cultural assemblage appeared in the Salt-Gila Basin. This assemblage was striking in that although it surfaced in a context suggesting a long and complex developmental sequence, local antecedents in the Salt-Gila Basin were lacking. A number of hypotheses have been proposed to account for the appearance of the Hohokam in southern Arizona, with most researchers (DiPeso 1956; Hayden 1970; Haury 1976) agreeing that the early cultural manifestations attributed to the Hohokam were the product of an immigrant group from Mexico. The exact time of this migration and the identity of the original immigrants still are disputed.

On the basis of his work at Snaketown, the type site for the River Hohokam, Haury (1976: 351-53) postulated that the Hohokam, who existed as a culturally distinct group prior to their migration, had colonized the Salt Gila Basin by about 300 B.C., bringing with them en bloc their previously developed cultural assemblage. Hayden (1970) agrees with this general interpretation, but has attempted to expand on it by specifying the identity of the immigrants. It is Hayden's opinion that the group today known as the Hohokam were descendants of the earlier Amargosan peoples who inhabited portions of northern or central Mexico in late Archaic times.

DiPeso has offered a somewhat different interpretation of those materials uncovered at Snaketown that Haury attributes to the Pioneer period Hohokam. DiPeso argues that pre-Colonial period remains in the Salt-Gila Basin are not Hohokam in origin, but were deposited by an indigenous group he identifies as Ootam. While agreeing with Hayden and Haury that the Hohokam were a migrant group who entered southern Arizona from Mexico, DiPeso (1956) feels that this migration did not occur until Colonial or early Sedentary period times. In the years following this migration, the indigenous Ootam culture of the Salt-Gila Basin was overshadowed and, in the end, dominated by the intrusive Hohokam culture.

Pioneer period remains are confined mainly to the Phoenix, Sacaton and Tucson areas of the Salt, Gila and Santa Cruz rivers (Haury 1976: 355); they occur later in the Santa Cruz than in the Salt-Gila Basin. While Pioneer period ceramics have been recovered as far west as the Gila Bend, no definite sites from this period have been identified in that area. Similarly, in the Santa Cruz Basin, Pioneer period remains are scanty and do not appear before A.D. 300 to 500.

The early Pioneer period is best documented by the excavations at Snaketown near the Gila River south of Phoenix. The earliest phase, the

Vahki phase, is recognized by a distinctive, large square pit house; plain brown and gray pottery; a distinctive red, polished ware; troughed metates; and cremation pit burials. In the succeeding Pioneer period phases the Hohoakm pit house becomes progressively smaller but retains a rectangular shape. The Estrella phase is distinguished by the important addition of painted pottery to the ceramic assemblage; the Sweetwater phase is distinguished by stylistic changes in pottery design. By the time of the Snaketown phase negative painting on pottery had been introduced and a lateral notch had appeared on projectile points (Haury 1965). Throughout the Pioneer period a general evolution toward elaboration in material culture items is seen in the increasing variety of non-utilitarian artifacts, such as carved bracelets, figurines and ornaments, and in an increasing complexity in pottery design.

In the Tucson Basin the earliest archaeological evidence of the Pioneer period consists of ceramics of the Sweetwater phase and of ceramics and pit houses of the Snaketown phase. Ceramics of these early phases occur in small quantities in the Tucson Basin, but are rarely associated with architecture. It is not until the Cañada del Oro phase (Colonial period) that the red-on-brown ceramic tradition supplants the red-on-buff ceramic tradition of the Gila Salt Basin in the Tucson Basin. The red-on-brown pottery exhibits polished surfaces, a close-grained paste, an absence of slip, the use of smudging and a tendency toward the use of more geometric designs. The use of some shapes and ornamentation characteristic of the Gila-Salt red-on-buff ware also is evident in the red-on-brown tradition. Because of the affinities between the Tucson Basin red-on-brown wares and the red-on-buff wares of the Gila-Salt Basin, the cultural chronology of the Tucson Basin was established to follow the chronology developed for the Gila-Salt Basin.

Colonial Period, A.D. 550-900. More is known of the Colonial period for both the Gila-Salt and Santa Cruz drainages. Excavations by Wasley and Johnson in the Gila Bend area (Wasley 1960; Wasley and Johnson 1961, 1965) and the surveys of Breternitz (1957), Schroeder (1952, 1961), and Vivian and Wasley (Vivian 1965) all point to a more intensive Hohokam occupation during the Colonial period; the Gila Bend area witnessed the establishment of permanent settlements along the Gila River extension of Hohokam settlements downstream to the Palomas Plains and a general increase in population. In the Tucson Basin, surveys along the Santa Cruz River and its tributaries (Grebinger 1971; Frick 1954) have recorded numerous late Colonial/early Sedentary (Rillito/Rincon phase) settlements, suggesting intensification of Hohokam settlement in this drainage. Expansion northward into the Agua Fria, New and Verde rivers, eastward up the Gila River to Safford, and southwest into the Papaguería occurs during this period (Haury 1976: 355).

In the lower Gila, Colonial period sites were located on the first and second terraces above the Gila River. The placement of villages at some distance from the river bed suggested to Wasley and Johnson (1965) that agricultural techniques employed by the River Hohokam of this period may have included the use of irrigation canals. It has been demonstrated by Cutler (Wasley and Johnson 1965) that maize was cultivated during the Colonial period in the Gila Bend area, and the work of Bohrer (1970) at Snaketown has demonstrated that beans, squash and cotton also were cultivated by the Colonial period Hohokam. Wild resources, both vegetal and faunal, supplemented cultivated foodstuffs in the diet.

The primary features observed at Colonial period sites along the lower Gila include oval domestic pit structures, surface storage structures, trash mounds and ball courts. The density and distribution of these remains suggests that the center of occupation along the lower Gila at this time was in the area between the Agua Caliente and Painted Rock mountains (Hayden 1972).

The Colonial period of the Gila-Salt Basin is marked by the appearance of new influences in the Hohokam cultural pattern. The Gila Butte phase is, at most, a transitional phase (Haury 1965: 256). All the features of the earlier Snaketown phase are present, but influences can be seen in the appearance of northern Arizona Anasazi pottery, changes in Hohokam pottery design, including conventionalization of old characters, addition of lifeforms and repetition of design elements. Cremations began to be placed in small pits instead of trenches. The major feature of this phase is the building of ball courts. In the later Santa Cruz phase, repeated elements reach their greatest popularity on the red-on-buff pottery. Also by this time, the Hohokam have developed a rich material culture, especially in shell items, such as rings, pendants and bracelets, and mosaic work, to name a few. A curious phenomenon associated with this phase is the presence of large trash mounds, which appear to demonstrate a deliberate building activity. Several explanations for these mounds have been suggested, although only a few have been tested.

In the Tucson Basin literature the Rillito phase of the late Colonial period and the Rincon phase of the Sedentary period usually are grouped for discussion, since they exhibit a great deal of continuity. For the purpose of clarity, these two phases will be discussed together in the section on the Sedentary period.

Sedentary Period, A.D. 900-1100. The close of the Colonial period at about A.D. 900 marks the beginning of the Sacaton phase of the Sedentary period. The Sacaton phase has been dated in the Gila Bend area at between A.D. 900 and 1150. This closing date does not correspond with the date given by Haury for the end of the Sedentary period at Snaketown (A.D. 1100). However, the presence of ceramic materials in apparently undisturbed Santa Cruz phase contexts dated elsewhere to about A.D. 1150 has led Wasley and Johnson (1965) to suggest that the Sedentary period may have lasted longer in the Gila Bend area than at Snaketown.

Cultural remains along the lower Gila and Salt-Gila Basin suggest that it was during the Sedentary period that the River Hohokam achieved their most elaborate level of cultural development and their greatest population density (Wasley and Johnson 1965: 51). While villages still were being built on terraces above the lower Gila River, domestic structures were constructed around large open plazas. There also are indications that a complex social organization was well developed by the Sacaton phase. The presence of large irrigation canals dating to this phase suggests cooperative efforts among community members. More ball courts appear to have been constructed during this period than at any other time, and the construction of a platform mound at the Gatlin Site indicates that a complex and internally cohesive social system was in operation.

In the Gila-Salt Basin the Sacaton phase is characterized by changes in architecture. The Hohokam pit house has become more of an above-ground structure, and houses generally are more carefully constructed; a greater refinement of detail is present and the shape is more elliptical, but the same basic form remains. A marked change is evident in pottery: instead of small vessels, the Hohokam began manufacturing huge jars, with a capacity of 30 or more gallons (Haury 1965). The distinctive Gila shoulder is added as a sharp angle at the greatest diameter. Copper bells are discovered in this phase and seem to indicate increasing contacts with other groups. Ball courts diminish in size, cremations in pits change to cremations in urns, and inhumation burial appears for the first time.

The Santan phase is not well represented nor understood. It is mostly recognized on the basis of Santan Red, a bright red pottery with a smoke-blackened interior. Houses of this phase are contiguous, sometimes enclosed within compound walls, a marked departure from the typical Hohokam dispersed rancheria-type settlement. It has been suggested that these traits may be derived from Salado influences filtering in from the Tonto Basin, where the Salado culture was forming at this time (Haury 1965: 264).

During the Rillito phase (late Colonial period) sedentary villages were established in the Tucson Basin along secondary drainages and, to a lesser extent, along primary drainages. The subsequent Rincon phase (Sedentary period) is characterized by settlements in both primary and secondary drainages. Frick's (1954) survey of the Santa Cruz Valley between Tubac and Sahuarita, though confined to readily accessible areas, suggests that settlement in this area reached its greatest density during the Rillito-Rincon phases. Of the 216 sites he recorded, the majority were Rillito-Rincon phase sherd and lithic scatters on the first or second terraces above the Santa Cruz River. A lower number of smaller surface scatters also occur at this time in the foothill zone. The limited number of excavations undertaken in the Santa Cruz Basin (Kelly 1978; DiPeso 1956; Hayden 1957; Greenleaf 1975a; Doyel 1977a) indicate that sites of this period range from small settlements (under 5,000 m^2 in area), such as the Baca Float sites (Doyel 1977a), to large 30-acre villages, such as Hodges. House types appear to be somewhat variable, ranging from quadilateral structures with rounded corners to ovoid structures; posthole arrangements also exhibit a wide range of variability. The indigenous decorated ceramics exhibit a basic continuity throughout Rillito-Rincon times, but Rincon Red-on-brown is distinguished from the earlier Rillito Red-on-brown by (1) a tendency toward thicker vessels, (2) new vessel shapes, (3) open design fields, (4) differences in color (Doyel 1977a: 31), and (5) a tendency toward geometric rather than curvilinear designs. By the close of the Sedentary period house styles changed from oval semi-subterranean and round jacal structures to subrectangular, slightly above-ground structures similar to those in the Gila-Salt Basin.

The nature of the late Colonial/early Sedentary (Rillito/Rincon) settlements (A.D. 700-1200) still is disputed. Grebinger (1971) and Doyel (1977b) have offered two different reconstructions of settlement, subsistence and social organization operating during the late Colonial/early Sedentary period. According to Grebinger (1971), subsistence was based on irrigation agriculture, which, in turn, supported a redistributive economy among hierarchically organized villages. The range of sites, from small farming settlements to large villages, and the differential distribution of luxury and trade goods among these villages would tend to support Grebinger's model; the scant evidence for ball courts and canals would tend to refute it. It should be noted, however, that the apparent absence of canals may be due to lack of investigation and to ground disturbance by cultivation in the flood plain during the historic period.

In contrast to Grebinger's model, Doyel (1977b) suggests that agriculture was based primarily on a variety of dry farming techniques practiced by the inhabitants of small, loosely knit, dispersed agricultural villages. Given a less dense, more dispersed population in what he terms a frontier setting, Doyel (1977b: 107) suggests that a greater emphasis was placed on flexibility rather than upon a complex social organization with status positions and leading villages. In this view, a lower level of social organization accounts for the general lack in the Tucson Basin of ball courts, platform mounds, carved stone and bone, pyrite mirrors, shell, copper bells, figurines and elaborate cremations, which are hallmarks of the Gila-Salt Basin Hohokam. Doyel's view of the differences between the middle Santa Cruz Basin and Gila-Salt Basin Hohokam resembles Haury's perspective on the Desert and River Hohokam. Doyel views the Hohokam as a flexible, widespread group with regional differences based on differing adaptations (in subsistence and social organization) to different habitats, and on differential contacts with other neighboring groups.

Of the two models, Doyel's (1977b) reconstruction seems to best explain the preponderance of small village sites and the general lack of some of the hallmarks of the Gila-Salt Basin Hohokam in the Tucson Basin; however, the evidence for confirming either model is lacking at this time. Systematic survey of the Pantano Wash and Rillito Creek, as well as systematic tests for canals in the flood plain, would help determine which model is accurate.

Classic Period, A.D. 1100-1450.   Archaeologists agree that the
Classic period is one of major cultural change for the River Hohokam, but
they differ in their interpretations of the causes of these changes. Widespread adjustments and changes in settlement pattern, subsistence pursuits
and material culture occur at the close of the Sedentary period.

Along the lower Gila the region of heaviest site density shifted
from the area between the Agua Caliente and Painted Rock mountains to the
Gila Bend area (Hayden 1972). Village sites located on terraces high
above the river were abandoned; Classic period villages (A.D. 1150-1450) were
situated on the flood plain itself or on the lower edges of the first
terrace. A major change in agricultural practices is suggested by the
abandonment of irrigation canals in the area. While agricultural practices
probably were not abandoned during this period, they apparently no longer
depended upon canal irrigation. Presumably, flood water farming became
the dominant mode of agricultural production. It also is possible that
dependence upon non-cultivated foodstuffs increased during the Classic
period. Occupation of the lower Gila area by the River Hohokam appears
to have ceased about A.D. 1450. The reasons for these shifts in settlement
patterning and agricultural practices have yet to be definitely established.
Schroeder (1961), however, has suggested that these shifts may have been
partly due to increasing desiccation after A.D. 900, and that desiccation
had reached the point by A.D. 1150 where irrigation agriculture no longer
was practicable.

Schroeder's interpretation of the Hohokam chronology in the lower
Gila area differs significantly from that proposed by Wasley and Johnson.
Like DiPeso, Schroeder (1960: 87-9) argues that the Hohokam cultural
pattern was not introduced into the Gila Basin until about A.D. 700, or
the beginning of the Colonial period. In a critique of Wasley and Johnson's
work in the Painted Rock Reservoir area, Schroeder (1967: 3-5) assumed
a more conservative stance and stated that there were no sites in the
reservoir area that could be unquestionably attributed to the Colonial
period Hohokam.

Schroeder's interpretation of Classic period events in the Salt-
Gila Basin and the lower Gila area also varies from that of Wasley and
Johnson. Schroeder (1960: 41) believes that the changes in the River
Hohokam cultural assembalge known to have occurred during the Classic
period in the Salt-Gila Basin are the result of an incursion of Sinagua
groups from the north. He argues that about A.D. 1150 the Hohokam and
Sinagua cultures in the Salt-Gila Basin merged, and that the Sinagua pattern dominated that of the Hohokam. Concerning the archaeology of the
lower Gila area specifically, Schroeder (1961) believes that there is
no evidence to support a Classic period Hohokam occupation. He believes
that the Hohokam abandoned the area by about A.D. 1150, and that the
cultural materials attributed by Wasley and Johnson to the Classic period
Hohokam occupation are in reality the product of Hakatayan occupation
that followed on the heels of Hohokam abandonment.

While there is not enough information available at present to accept or reject either hypothesis concerning the Hohokam chronology on the lower Gila, the cumulative results of the work of Wasley and Johnson (1965), Breternitz (1957), Vivian and Wasley (Vivian 1965) and Schroeder (1952, 1964, 1967) tend to support more strongly the conclusions of Wasley and Johnson than those of Schroeder.

Around A.D. 1150 a constellation of cultural traits foreign to the earlier Hohokam cultural pattern developed. Excavations at the Escalante Ruin Group (Doyel 1974), Classic period Hohokam sites east of Florence, Arizona, have yielded much data and new information regarding this period. Basically, traits manifested in the Santan phase and crystallized in the later Soho phase can be listed thus: extended inhumation burial, drastic changes in architectural styles (that is, post-reinforced surface dwellings and above-ground stone and mortar dwellings), and compound enclosures. At the Escalante Ruin Group, Doyel (1974: 188) notes that a major discernible difference between the Sacaton and Soho phases lies in the lithic assemblage, in which a large number of ornamental and not strictly utilitarian stone items occur in the Sacaton phase. By this time all burials are inhumations at Escalante.

During the Civano phase the material culture assemblage remains pretty much the same. The most outstanding feature is the continuing trend toward greater elaboration in architecture, best exemplified by the construciton of "great houses," such as at Casa Grande, and the building of contiguous room structures. Generally, what can be seen is a more formalized settlement pattern. The ceramic assemblage is characterized by a shift from red-on-buff pottery to the Saladoan Gila and Tonto polychromes as the dominant painted pottery. An increase in plainware vessel size also is apparent.

In the Salt-Gila Basin the Classic period is marked by the appearance of the following non-Hohokam elements: contiguous above-ground, adobe structures; compound enclosures; polychrome pottery, and extended inhumation and cremation burials. Numerous Salado sites occur in the vicinity of Globe, Arizona. Haury (1976: 355) views the appearance of the above traits as evidence of an intrusion of Salado peoples. However, Wasley (1966) and Doyel (1974) cite several lines of evidence indicating that the peculiar characteristics of the Classic period Hohokam may be better explained in terms of evolution from Hohokam traits present in the preceding Sacaton phase.

Similar changes have been noted in the Santa Cruz drainage. The early Classic period (Tanque Verde phase, A.D. 1200-1300) is characterized by the appearance of adobe-walled roughly rectangular structures and an infusion of puebloid design elements in local Tanque Verde Red-on-brown ceramics. Some evidence for the abandonment of villages also has been noted (Betancourt 1978: 18). During the subsequent Tucson phase (A.D. 1300-1500) contiguous, adobe-walled dwellings with compound walls, inhumation and polychrome pottery appear, and a shift in settlement to fewer, larger villages near major drainages occurs. Trincheras features (discussed below), such as those at Martinez Hill, Black Mountain and Tumamoc Hill, also are thought to date from the late Classic period.

Several theories have been posed to explain these dramatic changes in material culture in the Salt-Gila and Tucson basins. These include a migration from the Tonto Basin (Gladwin and others 1937; Haury 1976), the influence of pochteca (traders) from Mexico and a reorientation of trading centered on Casas Grandes, Mexico (Di Peso 1968), Sinagua migration from the Verde Valley (Schroeder 1960), and internal changes (Steen 1965; Wasley 1966). None of the current hypotheses has been thoroughly tested. While migration from the Tonto Basin traditionally has been favored as an explanation for changes in the Classic period, the information available is inadequate to demonstrate a large-scale movement of the Saladoans in either the Salt-Gila Basin or the Tucson Basin.

The Classic period ends around A.D. 1450 with the abandonment of large village settlements and the disappearance of the distinctive Salado elements. Haury suggests that Salado peoples withdrew from the Salt-Gila, leaving behind the residual Hohokam, who practiced a ranchería (or dispersed) settlement pattern similar to that known for the 19th century Papago. The reasons for this apparent withdrawal are not well understood.

Post-Classic, A.D. 1450-1700. Comparatively little is known of the years between the end of the Classic period and the arrival of the Spanish a century later. Three sites dating from this time have been excavated in the Santa Cruz Basin: the Palo Parado Ruin (DiPeso 1956), the England Ranch Ruin (AZ DD:8:129) and AZ DD:8:128, Locus B (Doyel 1977a). The latter two, characterized by oval to circular stone-lined structures on high bluffs or terraces above the river, are similar in configuration and location to a number of small sites recorded by Danson in his survey of the middle Santa Cruz drainage (Danson 1946; Doyel 1977a). Trough and slab metates, chipped stone, burned rock mounds and/or hearths, and small quantities of plainware pottery accompany these structures. Similar manifestations are reported in the San Pedro drainage and in the Santa Rita Mountains east and south of the Tucson Basin. Some of these sites in the San Pedro drainage are associated with historic Spanish items, leading DiPeso (1953) to suggest that these were Sobaipuri sites from the contact period. Based on similarities between his and DiPeso's sites, Doyel suggests that his own dated from A.D. 1500-1700, just prior to the contact period. He uses a more general term, Upper Pima, for the cultural affiliation of the sites, since direct evidence for a pre-contact Sobaipuri occupation is lacking. Sites from this period contain numerous small projectile points and a small quantity of ground stone, in contrast to the previous prehistoric periods. This suggests that the inhabitants were more dependent upon hunting and limited plant processing, although some agriculture is possible. The small, dispersed settlements, together with a limited inventory of material culture, are suggestive of a lower level of socio-cultural integration than that of the previous Classic period.

Desert Hohokam

According to Haury (1950: 547, 548), the Desert Hohokam practiced a mixed economy of gathering and dry and flood water agriculture in the region bounded by Chuichu on the north, the International Boundary on the south, Ajo on the west and the Avra Valley on the east. More recent excavations (Grebinger 1971) indicate that the Desert Branch extended further east into the Santa Cruz Basin. Haury's summary of the Desert Hohokam was based on investigations in the vicinity of Sells by Scantling (1940) and Withers (1941), who defined the Vamori, Topawa and Sells phases; the following discussion is based on Haury's summary.

Vamori Phase, A.D. 800-1100. The earliest ceramic occupation of the Papaguería is known from the excavation of Valshni Village (AZ DD:1:11); this occupation has been dated to the late Colonial/early Sedentary periods (A.D. 800-1100) on the basis of similarities (in intrusive red-on-buff ceramics, house types, village arrangements and luxury items) to those of the Santa Cruz and Sacaton phases at Snaketown. Intrusive Trincheras pottery and indigenous red-on-brown ceramics indicate additional ties with northern Sonora and the Tucson Basin, respectively. Very few sites of this phase have been discovered in the Papaguería, suggesting that this early ceramic occupation was a rather limited one.

Topawa Phase, A.D. 1100-1250. The Topawa phase, defined by excavations at Valshni Village and AZ BB:5:8, has been dated on the basis of intrusive Sacaton and Casa Grande Red-on-buff ceramics to the late Sedentary/early Classic periods (A.D. 1100-1250). As with the Vamori phase, Topawa phase domestic structures consist of surface or slightly excavated, oval or round, wattle and daub houses with east-facing entrances. The Topawa phase is distinguished from the later Sells phase by a lesser abundance of Sells Plain and a greater abundance of Valshni Red pottery. Few Topawa phase sites have been discovered to date. As shown in Table 2, Haury (1976) revised the dates for the end of the Sedentary period. If this new date is correct, this would probably push back the beginning dates for the Topawa phase but would not affect its end dates, since the end dates for the correlated Soho phase were not changed.

Sells Phase, A.D. 1250-1400. The late Desert Hohokam phase is known from excavations at Jackrabbit Ruin and Ash Hill, but published data are available only from Jackrabbit Ruin. The Sells phase is dated to A.D. 1250 to 1400 on the basis of Casa Grande Red-on-buff and Gila Polychrome sherds, and luxury goods (stone vessels, palettes, three-quarter grooved axes, mosaic plaques, and shell ornaments) similar to those of the Classic period at Snaketown.

Decorated ceramics reach a peak during the Sells phase. Tanque Verde Red-on-brown, the dominant decorated ware, indicates close ties with the Tucson Basin. According to Haury (1950), redware production increased sharply in the Sells phase, although an unexplained scarcity of redwares on Sells phase sites has been noted in recent investigations (Stacy 1974; Shenk and Coston n.d.; Rosenthal and others 1978; Vogler 1978). Compared with Valshni Village, Jackrabbit Ruin

yielded a smaller variety of mammal remains and a greater abundance
of ground stone, reflecting either a greater reliance upon cultivated
foods or a different season of occupation. Continuity with previous
phases is seen in house types, arts and crafts, and in the reliance
primarily upon wild foods.

While no Salado intrusion into the Papaguería occurred, the Sells
phase, like the late Classic period of the River Hohokam, seems to represent a departure from earlier times. Changes during the Sells phase
include a sharp increase in the number of Sells phase sites suggestive
of general population increase and/or changes in settlement and sub-
sistencence patterns; the construction of elevated platforms and
earthen enclosures reminiscent of Salado compound walls; and the
selection of easily defended locations for habitation and the construction
of trincheras features, possibly for defense purposes. Simple irrigation
systems (canals) associated with Sells phase ceramics occasionally have
been found in the Papaguería (Withers 1941: 9; Haury 1950: 15).

The Papaguería generally has been considered a marginal area
that exhibited a cultural lag. Recent radiocarbon dates from two
Sells phase (Classic period) sites (Rosenthal and others 1978) indicate
that the Sells phase may have started around A.D. 1100 rather than A.D.
1250. Whether this means that the Papaguería was not a lag area, whether
the dating of the River Hohokam sites is off, or whether the Sells phase
radiocarbon dates are unreliable is not known at this time.

Post-Classic, A.D. 1400-1700. Very little is known about Papaguería
archaeology for the period between the close of the Sells phase (A.D. 1400)
and the end of the 17th century, when Papago villages were first visited
by Kino. Haury presents several lines of evidence for a Desert Hohokam-
Papago continuum (Haury 1950: 520, 542-43). Recent surveys have produced
further evidence to suggest the validity of this linkage. Correlations
between late prehistoric sites and Papago field village locations were
noted. Site locations indicated a semiannual movement of late prehistoric
peoples similar to living patterns of the historic Papago (Stacy 1974).
Papago ceramic vessel shapes with Sells phase Tanque Verde designs and
the possible beginnings of the historic Papago projectile point type
are suggestive (Rosenthal and others 1978). Although the above evidence
is by no means conclusive, it does suggest that evidence for verifying
a continuum may exist.

To conclude this discussion of the Hohokam period, it should be
stressed that Haury's formulation of the relationship between the River
and Desert branches of the Hohokam remains a source of controversy, and
that other interpretations of the material in the archaeological record
have been offered by Hayden, Ezell and DiPeso. According to Haury, the
Papaguería was settled by groups from the Gila River, as evidenced by
the presence of many River Hohokam elements on Papaguería sites; differences between the Desert and River Hohokam are attributed to the different strategies required by riverine and desert settings. Unlike
Haury, Hayden stresses the differences between the Salt-Gila Basin on
the one hand, and between the Tucson Basin and the Papaguería on the

other. According to Hayden, the desert red-on-brown culture in the Papaguería and the Tucson Basin represents the development of local Amargosan groups who maintained Sonoran contact. The river dwelling red-on-buff culture was the result of the immigration of another Amargosan group from Mexico, who brought their already developed Pioneer period Hohokam culture intact with them (Hayden 1970: 90-92). Ezell (1954) also emphasizes the differences between the Hohokam buff-wares of the Salt-Gila Basin and the Sonoran brownwares of the Papaguería, and the affinities between the latter and Sonora, Mexico, an approach also followed by Rosenthal and others (1978). DiPeso contrasts groups that practiced canal irrigation and produced buffware pottery (the Salt-Gila Hohokam) with groups that practiced dry farming and produced red-on-brown ceramics (the Ootam). The latter are seen as indigenous groups inhabiting southern Arizona prior to the intrusion of dominant Salt-Gila immigrants. Valshni Village is an Ootam settlement, according to DiPeso (1956).

The interpretations by Hayden, Ezell, and DiPeso tend to equate ceramic cultures with social groups, and give less weight to the role of environmental differences in shaping subsistence strategies, social organization and material culture. The need for caution in interpreting ceramic materials is clearly seen in Doyel's investigations in the middle Santa Cruz Valley. Doyel (1977a: 105) notes that the many distinctions between buffwares and brownwares--vessel wall thickness, temper, paste color and consistency, and surface texture--may be due to differences in available raw materials, which mask the strong similarities in finishing and decorative techniques and in vessel form. More comparative analyses of entire assemblages are needed to clarify the political, economic and social ties between the Salt-Gila Basin, the Tucson Basin and the Papaguería.

Trincheras

One rather problematic culture manifestation found within and adjacent to the project area is the trincheras, or fortified hill, site. The term trincheras itself is confusing, in that it has been used to refer to a specific culture (Johnson 1963), to a ceramic complex (Hinton 1955) and to a particular type of site (Sauer and Brand 1931). Interpretive analyses of trincheras-type sites and the time period during which they were constructed or occupied remains unclear.

Trincheras sites are known to occur over much of southern Arizona, although the area with the highest density appears to be the Altar Valley in northern Sonora, Mexico. Trincheras sites in southern Arizona differ significantly from those encountered in northern Sonora in terms of their physiographic location and possibly in terms of their function and period of occupation. Sonoran trincheras almost invariably are associated with drainage systems, the highest density occurring in the drainages of the Magdalena and Altar rivers. These sites usually occur close to open valley floors. They are characterized by Trincheras Purple-on-red and Trincheras Polychrome ceramics, rock corrals or enclosures, and series of man-made terraces situated on the slopes of hills (Johnson 1963; Sauer and Brand 1931).

The function of these hill top sites is unknown, but it has been hypothesized that they served as defensive sites, habitation sites or agricultural sites. There are problems with each of these interpretations. While many of the Sonoran trincheras sites contain considerable evidence for occupation, possibly over an extended period of time, there are many that do not. There is not enough data presently available to make definitive statements concerning the relative density of domestic structures at these fortified sites, although there appear to be relatively few domestic structures at the fortified sites when compared with sites of the same cultural affiliation on nearby valley floors.

It is possible that the terraced slopes found at many trincheras sites served as agricultural plots; again, however, insufficient data are available at this time to make any clear-cut statement in this regard. It is interesting to note that most of these Sonoran sites occur immediately above large tracts of alluvial deposits, areas which would seem much more suitable for agricultural activities than would the steep slopes of the trincheras hills.

The functional interpretation that appears to have received the most attention and support in trincheras literature is that they were constructed to provide defense against enemies. The Pima and Seri in northern Sonora are known to have occupied trincheras sites during their revolt against the Spanish, as did the Apache during their raiding adventures into Sonora (Johnson 1963; Sauer and Brand 1931). In both cases, however, the groups involved were occupying trincheras sites that had previously been occupied and then abandoned. It has not yet been determined whether these sites served the same defensive function in prehistoric times.

Sonoran trincheras sites on the valley floor or the lower terraces appear to be habitation sites and often contain almost no intrusive ceramic materials. Many of the trincheras sites surveyed by Hinton in the Altar Valley contained almost 100 percent trincheras ceramic wares, which suggests that the occupants of these sites lived within a rather closed cultural system when compared to groups occupying the Gila or Salt river areas. Hinton (1955: 6) noted during the course of his survey that while rock trincheras were found on practically every suitable hill in the valley, trincheras ceramics were rare at such sites, most of the pottery present being either late Gila Plain or Altar Plain. He concluded that these rock trincheras probably were pre-contact Pima sites, whose construction post-dated the occupation of the group that produced the trincheras pottery so common at sites on the valley floor (Hinton 1955: 6). Johnson (1963) has suggested that the trincheras sites in northern Sonora are attributable to a distinct cultural group that occupied the area between A.D. 800 and 1100. While he makes no statement concerning the specific cultural or ethnic identity of this group, he does remark that its cultural manifestations closely parallel those of the Desert Hohokam (Johnson 1963: 174-75). Johnson arrived at his dates for the culture through the identification of intrusive ceramics at trincheras sites previously identified in the Gila Basin.

Pheriba Stacy in 1974 conducted a study of five trincheras sites in the Baboquivari Valley in the Papaguería. The results of her study differ significantly from those carried out in Sonora, Mexico. Ceramics recovered by Stacy firmly placed the period of occupation for all five sites between A.D. 1200 and 1400. Stacy found no evidence to support the hypothesis that the hill top sites had served as areas of extended occupation, although there were indications that intermittent, short-term occupation might have occurred. She did note, however, that in every case a large habitation site was located in the immediate vicinity of the trincheras site and that it apparently dated to the same period as the trincheras (Stacy 1974). Stacy also observed that the location of the trincheras sites in her study area did not correspond with the location of trincheras sites in Sonora, in that the Arizona sites were situated in non-riverine contexts.

Papago informants stated that the trincheras were Papago sites used by the Papago as defensive fortifications during the time of Apache raids in the area. Stacy found no evidence that the sites dated later than A.D. 1400, much too early to have been constructed as defenses against Apache raiders. Stacy has suggested that the Baboquivari Valley trincheras probably served specialized defensive, and possibly agricultural, functions as satellite components of larger permanent habitation sites in the vicinity (Stacy 1974).

The Fortified Hill Site near Gila Bend, Arizona is a trincheras site occupied between A.D. 1200 and 1300. The site is particularly significant, in that it seems to have been during this period that the site was equipped with defensive features, a series of walls that separate the main village complexes from open portions of the mesa top on which it is located (Greenleaf 1975b). The cultural identity of the group that occupied the mesa top site appears to have been Tucson Basin Hohokam, although the question has not been completely resolved. In any case, it appears that the village was constructed with its defense as a primary concern.

While it is impossible at this time to state categorically the function of trincheras sites in the Papaguería, it is interesting to note that the period during which it is thought trincheras sites were occupied (A.D. 1200 to 1400) corresponds with Schroeder's hypothesized Sinagua invasion of the Salt-Gila Basin (Schroeder 1960: 41) and with the infusion of Salado elements in the Salt-Gila and Tucson basins (Gladwin and others 1937: 265; Betancourt 1978: 20). The hypothesized influx of Piman-speaking Sobaipuri about A.D. 1450 (Schroeder 1960) also is very close in time to the period of trincheras occupation. The possible connections between these two disruptive cultural episodes and the construction and occupation of trincheras sites in the Papaguería merit consideration by researchers working in the area in the future.

Hakatayan (Yuman)

In addition to the Hohokam, another major cultural group iden-tified as Yuman by early researchers, has a long occupational history in southwestern Arizona. Objections have been raised (Schroeder 1960) to the application of the term Yuman to prehistoric cultural remains, as the term Yuman originally referred to a historic language group. The objections rest on the fact that it has not been demonstrated that all prehistoric desert cultures that have in the past been labeled Yuman are related to historic Yuman groups. The result is that the use of the term for pre-historic materials implies a direct relationship between historic and prehistoric groups. Schroeder (1960) has suggested that the term Hakatayan be applied to that group of traits basic to all Yuman cultures on the lower Colorado River and in west-central Arizona in prehistoric ceramic times. With the aim of minimizing the possibility of con-fusing historically documented groups with groups that are known archaeologically, Schroeder's suggestion is followed here.

Just when the first Hakatayan groups emerged on the scene in the vicinity of the study area is uncertain. Malcolm Rogers, operating within the Yuman terminological framework, has suggested that Yuman groups drifted eastward into the Colorado River Valley from southern California about A.D. 800 (Rogers 1945: 169). Work later carried out by Schroeder indicates that the Hakatayan culture appeared in the Gila Basin area about A.D. 700, where it was dominated by the local Hohokam tradition (Schroeder 1960: 87). Regardless of the date of emergence of the Hakatayan pattern, the lower Colorado Basin and the lower Gila Basin both have failed to produce an intervening cultural developmental sequence between the last hunting complexes of these areas and the subsequent Hakatayan ceramic complexes.

The emergence of an identifiable Hakatayan cultural tradition is marked by the appearance of a number of characteristic traits. Those groups which settled along the lower Colorado and lower Gila rivers adopted a subsistence strategy based on flood water agriculture, wild food gathering and the hunting of small game (Rogers 1945; Schroeder 1957).

Riverine villages consisted of individual household units scattered
in an unstructured arrangement. Domestic structures initially consisted of rock-encircled, round or oval, domed jacal structures without
roof supports. This type of structure was later replaced by square
structures of jacal with four roof supports. Settlements located away
from the riverine environment maintained the unstructured internal
arrangement of domestic units, but the houses were of the circular,
domed jacal type throughout the cultural sequence. A common feature
at Hakatayan sites is the presence of large quantities of fire-cracked
rock, the remains of stone-lined roasting pits. Hakatayan ceramics
were predominantly plainwares and brown and red types decorated with
red paint (Schroeder 1957, 1960).

Individuals attempting to reconstruct Hakatayan prehistory are
handicapped by several factors. Riverine Hakatayan groups tended
to establish their settlements on the flood plain or on islands in
the river channel. Recent agricultural activities and natural geologic processes acting upon the river courses have destroyed many of
these sites. Researchers often have been forced to obtain most of their
data on early Hakatayan occupation from outside the river valleys,
which results in an unavoidably biased analysis. The dearth of
cultural materials at most Hakatayan sites, many of which consist of
little more than fire-cracked rock and a few sherds, poses yet another
problem.

It often has been the case that the identification of sites
as Hakatayan has rested solely upon the presence or absence of
ceramic materials attributed to this group (Breternitz 1957; Vivian
1965). The problem with this approach is that there is considerable
disagreement among researchers as to the cultural affiliation of some
of the ceramic types in question, particularly along the lower reaches
of the Gila River. It is for these reasons that no detailed reconstruction
of Hakatayan prehistory can be offered. It is possible, however, to
suggest a generalized reconstruction of Hakatayan prehistory based
on what limited information is available today.

With the initial migration of Hakatayan groups out of southern
California and into southwestern Arizona sometime between A.D. 700
and 800, semi-permanent settlements were established along the lower
Colorado and lower Gila rivers. A new subsistence pattern was adopted
as agricultural activities began to be pursued and the production of
ceramics was undertaken for the first time. Archaeological evidence
indicates that in these early times the greatest development of
material culture among the Hakataya occurred near the confluence of
the Gila and Colorado rivers (Rogers 1945).

The history of Hakatayan groups between A.D. 800 and about 1300
is unclear. Wasley and Johnson (1965) cite evidence from the Painted
Rock area that suggests to them that the lower Gila in the vicinity of
Gila Bend was occupied contemporaneously by both the Hohokam and Hakatayan

groups during the Classic period, and possibly as early as the Sedentary period. If their interpretation is correct, Hakatayan occupation of the Gila Bend area could have begun as early as A.D. 900. Schroeder, however, interprets the same archaeological materials as indicating that Hakatayan occupation of the Gila Bend area did not begin until after the Hohokam occupation had ceased, approximately A.D. 1150 (Schroeder 1961, 1967). Ceramics recovered from sites downstream from Gila Bend demonstrate that there was considerable contact between Hohokam and Hakatayan groups along the lower Gila, whether or not these two groups shared portions of the same occupational range.

It is known that at about A.D. 1300 much of the territory occupied by Hakatayan groups was abandoned and the last major Hakatayan expansion occurred. A group Schroeder has identified as the Gila Bend branch of the Hakataya (known historically as the Opa) migrated upstream along the Gila to the Gila Bend area at approximately A.D. 1300. This migration appears not to have affected the social organization of the group, as the settlement patterns and subsistence activities employed in their former territory continued to characterize the new Gila Bend settlements. Schroeder (1960: 5, 102) has suggested that a breakdown or replacement of the established Hakatayan culture occurred in the Gila Basin at the end of the Classic period, with historic Pima cultural patterns being introduced into the area about A.D. 1450.

Considerable attention has been given to the problem of determining the ethnic identities of populations known to have inhabited the Colorado and Gila basins in early historic times. A number of researchers, working from archaeological and ethnographic sources and early historic documents, have proposed hypotheses concerning the origins of those groups encountered in the study area by the early Spanish explorers. Schroeder (1960) has proposed the following explanatory model. The Laquish "stem" of the Hakatayan cultural pattern, which represents riverine Hakatayan manifestations, includes a number of separate archaeological "branches." These archaeological branches gave rise to the historic groups occupying the lower Colorado and lower Gila area during early post-contact times. Schroeder (1960: 97-98) proposes the following cultural continua:

Archaeological Branch	(gave rise to)	Historic Group
Palo Verde		Yuma
Amacava		Mohave
Gila Bend		Maricopa
Lower Gila		Opa
La Paz		Halchedoma

Documentary sources provide considerable information relative to the distribution of Hakatayan groups during the 19th century. Prior to 1800, the Gila Basin north of Gila Bend was occupied by the Maricopa (the Cocomaricopa of early Spanish records). The area around Gila Bend

and lands downstream about halfway to the Colorado River were occupied
by the Kaveltcadom (the Opa of early Spanish records) (Spier 1933).
That portion of the lower Gila between the Colorado River and the
western end of the Kaveltcadom range was occupied by the Yuma (Rogers 1936).

The term Maricopa was used in the latter half of the 19th century
to refer to all Yuman-speaking peoples of the Gila River area, and
this indiscriminate use of the term has resulted in considerable con-
fusion in recent literature (Ezell 1963a). For the purposes of this
report, the term is meant to refer only to that group of Native Americans
who occupied the Gila Basin north of Gila Bend during early post-contact
times, and their historic descendants.

About 1825 the Kaveltcadom left the territory they had been
occupying in early post-contact times and migrated east, eventually
merging with the Maricopa. The Maricopa depended largely on the
gathering of wild foodstuffs, fishing and the hunting of small game
for their subsistence base. Although corn, beans, cotton, blackeyed
peas, pumpkins and watermelons were cultivated, cultigens did not
constitute the bulk of the vegetal elements in the Maricopa diet; wild
foodstuffs, particularly mesquite beans, served this function (Spier 1933).

Pima

Considerable attention has been given to the question of a possible
Hohokam-Pima cultural continuum in the Gila Basin (Ezell 1963b; Haury 1976;
Schroeder 1960). Noting the apparent disruption of the established
cultural manifestations in the Gila Basin at about A.D. 1450, Schroeder
(1960) has hypothesized that a Piman-speaking Sobaipuri group overran
the inhabitants of the Gila-Salt Basin in the 15th century. This influx
of Sobaipuri into the area resulted in the introduction of the Pima cultural
pattern, producing the complex identified historically as Gila-Pima. If
Schroeder's reconstruction of events in the area is correct, it argues
against a Hohokam-Pima cultural continuum. Ezell (1963b) and Haury (1976)
feel, however, that there is very strong evidence to indicate that such
a continuum did exist. Pioneer period Hohokam architectural features
closely resemble those of later Pimans. Trends in pottery designs can
be traced through late Hohokam ceramics which suggest a close relationship
with motifs appearing on later Piman vessels. Perhaps the strongest
support for a Hohokam-Pima continuum can be drawn from the agricultural
practices of the two groups. The Hohokam practiced canal irrigation
techniques in the Salt and Gila valleys. Although several groups who
occupied the Salt-Gila Basin during early post-contact times practiced
agriculture, all of them, with the exception of the Pima, were totally
dependent upon flood water farming for the success of their crops. It
was the Pima alone, among all of the groups of the Basin, who practiced
irrigation agriculture in post-contact times (Ezell 1963b).

Significant differences between the Hohokam and Pima cultures must be recognized. The Pima burial practice of inhumation is in no way comparable to the Hohokam tradition of cremation. The Pima lacked knowledge of the use of metal, did not construct ball courts and lacked a history of work in shell and stone, traits for which the Hohokam are noted. But, as Ezell points out, the Pima did not exist in a cultural vacuum; neither did the Hohokam. It is known that both groups had considerable contact with Hakatayan groups to the west. What is unknown at this time is whether these contacts, or contact with still other groups, were of sufficient magnitude to have sparked the changes seen between the Hohokam of the Pioneer period and the later Piman occupants of the Salt-Gila Basin.

According to Schroeder (1952), Kino in 1694 reported a number of Sobaipuri (an eastern Piman group) rancherías on the San Pedro River and six or seven rancherías around Casa Grande on the Gila River. This account is the earliest known document referring specifically to the Pima, who impressed Kino with their friendliness and hospitality. Since 1700, the Pima have inhabited at least two areas in southern Arizona. Most lived in the Santa Cruz River Valley near Tucson and Red Rock; others occupied areas on the Gila River near Sacaton. According to Spier (1933: 7) sometime prior to 1880 Apache groups drove the Santa Cruz group northwest, where they joined the Sacaton group. In 1859 the first reservation was established for the Pima and Maricopa (a Yuman group), which included all of the villages from Casa Blanca to immediately west of Pima Butte (Hayden 1965).

Papago

The Papago and the Gila River Pima are the only two Piman groups that have retained their separate, tribal identities. Haury (1950: 18) has suggested a possible linkage between the Desert Hohokam and historic Papago. The following summary of the Papago is drawn from Hackenberg (1962, 1964), who used historic accounts, informants and ethnographic sources in his study. This information pertains primarily to the Papago who occupied central Papaguería, a southern Arizona region bounded by the Gila River, the Ajo Mountains and the Baboquivari Mountains, and roughly equivalent to the Desert Hohokam region defined by Haury (1950).

Little is known of the protohistoric and early historic periods. Papago houses, built from local materials on the surface or excavated to a depth of two feet, were dome-shaped pole structures. Other structures included ramadas and temporary semi-circular brush shelters (Fontana 1964: 38, 39). Figures 3, 4, 5, and 6 illustrate the variety of Papago house types. Papago crafts include, among other items, baskets and pottery (Fontana 1964: 55-61), the latter consisting mainly of two redwares: one with a dense black core, the other a light red with white temper in a brown matrix. Decorated types include red-on-buff, white-on-buff, black-on-red and glazed. A diagnostic Papago projectile point is

Figure 3. Papago Indian house covered with ocotillo stalks, possibly near Vamori, 1894. Courtesy Arizona State Museum, The University of Arizona Archives, Photograph No. 2050. Photographer: William Dinwiddie, Bureau of American Ethnology.

Figure 4. Papago Indian house and possible "pottery manufacturing place" at Pitiquito, Sonora, 1894. Courtesy Arizona State Museum, The University of Arizona Archives, Photograph No. 2033. Photographer: William Dinwiddie, Bureau of American Ethnology.

Figure 5. Papago Indian house made of willow boughs possibly in Sycamore Canyon, 1894. Courtesy Arizona State Museum, The University of Arizona Archives, Photograph No. 2082. Photographer: William Dinwiddie, Bureau of American Ethnology.

Figure 6. Papago Indian house of grass with posts for defense against wild and domesticated animals at Vamori Village, 1894. Courtesy Arizona State Museum, The University of Arizona Archives, Photograph No. 2078. Photographer: William Dinwiddie, Bureau of American Ethnology.

small and triangular with a concave base (Haury 1950: 341, 346, 350-51).
Castetter and Bell (1942: 47-58) projected that before the Spanish
arrival, the ratio of gathered plants and animals to cultivated plants
was four to one, with a similar ratio between native plants and wild
animals. Historically, hunting and gathering maintained its dominance,
amounting to 75 percent of Papago subsistence (Hackenberg 1962: 188).
Hackenberg has compiled a list of native plants and animals used by
the Papago. During hard times the use of wild resources became more
extensive. Hackenberg also provided a list of plants cultivated by
the Papago, including native and introduced domestics. The only
domestic animals were the dog and certain birds kept for their
feathers; the Spanish arrival introduced other domestic species
(Hackenberg 1964: 11-38, 56). Cattle did not become an important
industry for the Papago until the last quarter of the 19th century
(Hackenberg 1964: IV-129).

Documentary sources indicate that during the 19th century the
Papago in the central Papaguería migrated on a seasonal basis between
small dispersed "field" and "well" villages. While the description
below is based primarily upon 19th century information, it is generally
thought that this limited migratory settlement pattern also prevailed
in the 17th and 18th centuries; the fact that many 19th century villages
have been identified as settlements visited by Kino between 1695 and
1700 supports this contention (Underhill 1939: 60-69).

During the summer rainy season (July through September) the Papago
occupied temorales, or field villages, on the alluvial flats of a major
intermittent wash on the valley floor. Here, flood water (ak chin) farming,
sometimes aided by the construction of earthen dikes and water storage
tanks, was undertaken. Charcos were dug as temporary sources of domestic
water. With the field villages as a base, women would gather nearby
wild resources, such as pig-weed, mesquite beans and goosefoot. Women
from a number of field villages also would set out from the summer
settlements to harvest wild potato, cholla and prickly-pear fruits,
palo-verde beans, peppers and acorns from the bajadas of the nearby
mountains. Wild grass seeds probably were harvested late in the
summer; their contribution to the Papago diet is a matter of conjecture,
since there is little agreement on the extent of Papaguería grasslands
prior to the 1880s.

With the end of the summer rains people began the return to small
well villages near permanent springs and tanks in the bajadas. These
small water sources limited the size of the village to one or two extended
families. During the winter months the women manufactured house-hold
items, such as baskets, pottery vessels and clothing; in post-contact
times leather harness also was manufactured at this season. Early in
the winter men collected the more distant plant resources while on
hunting and trading missions; such bajada and mountain resources as
agave, sotol, Papago bluebells and wild onion became important elements
of the winter diet. In the early spring cholla buds and joints were
collected in the vicinity of the well villages.

Temporary campsites are the third type of settlement known from ethnographic accounts. Campsites ranged from briefly occupied individual hunting encampments to family camps occupied for several weeks, perhaps on an annual basis, for the purpose of collecting and processing nearby plant foods, such as saguaro fruits or acorns. Saguaro camps, the best documented of the temporary settlements, consisted of a ramada built on a saguaro-bearing mountain slope and a few portable items, such as a water jar, a cooking pot and a metate, for collecting and processing. All usable utensils usually were carried away when harvesting ended (Stacy 1974: 78). While these sites exist in the archaeological record, they can be easily overlooked.

During the contact period, the Papago participated to a degree in the non-Indian economy. Documentary evidence indicates that 18th century Papagos obtained placer gold in the Ajo Mountains and sold it in Caborca, Mexico. During the 19th century some Papagos migrated on a seasonal basis to harvest for Mexican farmers; some sought employment in mines near Tucson, Tubac and Ajo and on ranches in Mexico when village tanks dried up. Some served as army scouts; still others gathered salt from playas on the Papaguería and marketed it in Tucson and Tubac. Papagos also initiated their own mining and ranching ventures in the latter half of the 19th century (Hackenberg 1964: IV, 111-29). This participation in the non-Indian pioneer economy apparently did not alter Papago settlement and subsistence; rather, selected European elements were added to the range of exploitable resources in a manner that allowed traditional patterns to persist.

Unlike European contact, Apache raiding between 1768 and 1870 did influence Papago settlement patterns, although the exact effects on the Papaguería between 1830 and 1870 remain disputed. Certain effects are well established. By 1768 Apache raids drove the Sobaipuri (a Piman-speaking group) from the San Pedro Valley to the Santa Cruz Valley. A century later the Papago/Apache boundary had shifted westward to the Baboquivari Mountains, with raiding parties ranging as far south as Sonoita, Mexico, and west to Ajo (Hackenberg 1964: IV-124, V-4). A Papago calendar stick in the Arizona State Museum recorded that in 1850 the Apaches destroyed Batki (Kui Tatk), a Papago village approximately 8 miles northwest of present-day Sells (Haury 1950: 19-20). After the cessation of Apache raids in 1870, Papago field and well villages were established in areas of the eastern Papaguería that were devoid of settlements in the mid-19th century.

Whether Apache raids displaced Papago settlements to the western half of the Papaguería or simply delayed the founding of new "daughter" villages has not been established. According to Mark (cited in Hackenberg 1964: IV-106), Papagos were forced to locate almost all field and well villages in the western Papaguería west of 112 degrees longitude. Hackenberg cites additional evidence for the deliberate selection of village locations away from tanks and springs frequented by Apaches crossing the Papaguería, both to avoid the Apaches and to allow Papagos a clear field for pursuit if the Apaches attacked (Hackenberg 1964: IV-80).

During this period Papagos were organized in so-called "defense" villages, which served to concentrate field and well villages so that sufficient numbers could be mustered to fight on short notice.

Studies by Underhill (1939: 60-69), however, support the view that raiding delayed the normal "budding off" of daughter villages but did not cause a substantial relocation of villages. Underhill identified the 11 19th century "defense" villages in the central Papaguería (Table 3) as settlements visited by Kino at the end of the 17th century; this indicates that there was considerable stability in Papago settlement patterns despite Apache raiding. Archaeological survey in the eastern portion of the Papaguería should clarify the effect of Apache raids on Papago settlements.

Table 3. Nineteenth Century "Defense" Villages [1,2]

Drainage	Village Name
San Simon	Kaka
	Perigua (Hickiwan)
	Gue Va (Gu Vo)
Vamori Wash[3]	Kupk
	Kui Tatk (Batki)
	Komalik (Komelik)
	Tecolote (Chukut Kuk)
Santa Rosa Wash	Santa Rosa (Gu Achi)
	Ak Chin
	Anegam
	Quajote (Kohatk)
Unnamed drainage basin which flows toward Gulf of California	Quitovac[4] (Mexico)

1. Compiled from Hackenberg (1964: IV, 87-89).

2. Underhill (1939: 60-69) cited by Hackenberg (1964: IV-89), indicates that these villages in the San Simon, Vamori, and Santa Rosa washes were settled by the late 17th century, the time of Kino's visits.

3. Includes an unnamed wash parallel to Vamori Wash and Gu Oidak, Baboquivari, and Fresnal washes, tributaries to Vamori Wash, which in turn, flows into San Simon Wash.

4. Quitovac is outside the central zone, some 30 miles south of Sonoita, Sonora, Mexico.

The establishment of new field and well villages east of 112 degrees longitude, initiated in the mid-19th century, accelerated when Apache raids ceased in the 1870s. This village expansion, summarized in Table 4, is discussed below in greater detail for the area immediately west of the Baboquivari Mountains.

Before the mid-19th century most of the Baboquivari Valley was unoccupied, with the exception of the field village of Komalik in the Vamori drainage and an associated complex of well villages near Fresnal Canyon at the foot of the Baboquivari Mountains. The latter villages, located in a well known Spanish and Mexican mining district, may predate the Gadsden Purchase and definitely were occupied as early as 1863 (Hackenberg 1964: IV-100, 123). Soon thereafter Komalik inhabitants established two new field villages, Choulic and Topawa, in the Vamori drainage, and additional well villages in the Fresnal Canyon area.

It was reported in 1861 that Papagos were raising cattle and horses in the southern end of the Baboquivari Valley near the Pozo Verde Mountains, a location that was reported to be abandoned in 1855 and 1864 (Hackenberg 1964: IV-115, 124). Between 1875 and 1900 four villages related to Tecolote (Chukut Kuk) in the Vamori drainage were established in the Baboquivari Valley just north of the International Boundary. These were the field villages of Hashan Chuchg, Buenos Aires and San Miguel, and a well village, Sapano Vaya, related to San Miguel.

Settlement in the northern portion of the Baboquivari Valley dates as early as 1863 (with the establishment of Pan Tak, a daughter village related to the Kui Tatk complex) (Hackenberg 1964: IV-123); however, the major expansion in this region post-dates 1875. During the expansion period, Haivana Nakya and Viopuli were established as field villages. Well villages were established at Pavo Kug and at Gu Chiapo and Chiawuli Tak in and near the Baboquivari Mountains. A complex of villages also was established in and near the Comobabi Mountains, a 19th century mining district; these included the well villages of Koson Vaya, Rincon, Nawt Vaya and Ko Vaya, and the field villages of Nolia, San Luis and Not Tak. In the Artesa Mountains, Indian Oasis (present day Sells) and the related Papago village of Artesa were settled by 1910 by groups affiliated with Kui Tatk and Tecolote. Many of these post-1875 villages were established near abandoned mining and cattle operations where wells had been dug.

The San Xavier and Gila Bend Indian Reservations were set aside for the Papagos in 1874 and 1882, respectively. The rest of the Papaguería remained in the public domain (and therefore open to Anglo mining and ranching) until 1916, when the Sells Reservation was established; the reservation was expanded in 1931 to its present boundaries. In 1914 the federal government began digging permanent wells and improving stock tanks and reservoirs. As a result of this program many field and well villages had become permanent settlements by 1933.

TABLE 4

Parent and Daughter Villages

Parent or Defense Village	Villages Associated with Parent Village				Daughter Villages		
	Well	Field	Defense	Unknown	Well	Field	Unknown
Kaka (field)	Moi Vaya prior to 1870		Ahak Owuch pre 1870		Ventana-20th Vaya Chin-20th Muik Vaya-20th	Gila Bend-1870s Maricopa Ak Chin 1870s	
Hickiwan (field)	Chiulikam Sikort Chuapo mid 19th Stoa Vaya-mid 19th	Stoa Pitk-mid 19th			Schuchuli-20th	Emika-1870+ Tatia Toak-1870s+ Hotason Vo-20th	
Gue Va (Gu Vo) (field)	Chiulikam				Tonoka-late 19th Kuakatch-20th	Chagit Vo-20th	
Kupk (field)	San Antone	Komak Wuacho-17th Ahah Owuch "ancient"			Stoa Vaya-mid 19th well village for at least four field villages Piato Vaya	Pisinimo-mid 19th Hali Murk-mid 19th Chiuli Vo-mid 19th Kom Vo-mid 19th Cowlic-20th Vopolo Havoka-20th Tatk Kam Vo-20th Viason Chin-20th Kui Chut Vachk Chuwut Murk	

Table 4 (continued)

Villages Associated with Parent Village

Parent or Defense Village	Well	Field	Defense	Unknown	Daughter Villages Well	Field	Unknown
Kui Tatk (well)	Suwuki Chuapo 19th	Gu Oidak-17th Not Tak-19th		Vainom Kug mid 19th Kaihon Kug mid 19th	Pavo Kug-late 19th Koson Vaya-late 19th Rincon-late 19th Gu Chuapo late 19th Nawt Vaya late 19th Uhs Kug-late 19th Ko Vaya(Cababi) Artesa (Sells)--settled also by Tecolote peoples early 20th	Pan Tak-mid 19th Havana Nakya-mid 19th Viopuli-mid 19th Chiawuli Tak-late 19th Nolia-late 19th San Luis-late 19th	Gukawo Ki "recent"
Komalik (Baggiburi) (field)	Chutum Vaya				Kom Kug Pitoikam and 25 other wells of the Fresnal Canyon Complex-pre mid 19th San Juan Spring Chui Vaya-by 20th Gu Kui Chuchg-by 20th	Choulic-mid 19th Topawa-19th Ali Chukson-19th Ali Monila-19th	
Tecolote (field)	Cobabi, Mexico-19th Stan Shuatak-20th Ak Komelik "old"	Sivili Chuchg "old"			Haivan Vaya-1875-1900 Sapano Vaya-1875-1900 Ak Chut Vaya "early"	Vamori-1875-1900 San Miguel-1875-1900 Buenos Aires-1875-1900 Hashan Chuchg-1875-1900 San Rafael "early"	

Table 4 (continued)

Parent of Defense Village	Villages Associated with Parent Village				Daughter Villages		
	Well	Field	Defense	Unknown	Well	Field	Unknown
Santa Rosa (Gu Achi Complex) (field)	Kom Vaya-"early" Sil Nakya-"early" Ko Vaya-"early" Noipa Kam-"early" Quijotoa-"early" Maish Vaya-"early" Chot Vaya-19th	Achi-17th Gu Achi-17th Ali Oidak-17th San Serafin-17th				Sikul Himatk mid-19th Gurli Put Vo mid-19th Makgum Havcka mid-19th Ahi Vonam post mid-19th Logan-post mid-19th Oit Ihuk-recent	Skoksonik "recent" post-WWI
Anegam (field)	Omik Vaya by mid-19th				Chiapuk-post 1850 Gu Komelik-post-1885		
Quajote (Kohatk) (field)	Sif Vaya "ancient"		Totopitk-by mid-19th Chuichu-by mid-19th Vaiva Vo-by mid-19th Shopishk-by mid-19th				Tat Momoli-post 1880s
Quitovac (field)		Ali Ak Chin mid-late 19th Shaotkam mid-late 19th		Taak (La Nariz) El Mezquite-by 1850			Pia Oik-late 19th Siovi Shuatak- late 19th Ali Chuk-ca. 1930 Suwuki Tonk-ca. 1930 Sikort Wuacho-ca. 1930

Areneños

The western area of the Papaguería, including southwestern
Arizona and northwestern Sonora, was occupied historically by
Areneños--variously called Sand Papago, Soba, Hiatit Ootam (Fontana
1965: 99)--a dialect group of the Papago. Ethnographic work was not
done with these Indians before the area was abandoned; available
information is based on historic accounts, informants and ethnographic data from elsewhere in the Papaguería. Conflicting information
exists on the exact range of the Areneños, particularly regarding their
eastern boundary (Rosenthal and others 1978; Ezell 1954: 367; Fontana
1965: 100; Hackenberg 1964: 11, 28-9; Hayden 1970: 87), but is appears
that they ranged from the lower Gila River south to Caborca, Sonora,
and from the lower Colorado River to at least just east of the Ajo
Mountains in the southwest corner of the present-day Sells Papago
Indian Reservation.

There apparently were two bands of Areneños (Fontana 1965: 99-
101; Hayden 1967, 1970, 1972); the following description is based
on Fontana and Hayden. One band, which Hayden has termed the Areneños
Pinacateños, was based in the Sierra Pinacates. These nomadic hunters
and gatherers did not farm or make their own pottery. They relied
on wild plants and animals, including marine life from the Gulf of
California, and possibly on some farm produce obtained by trade with
Yumans of the lower Colorado River, from whom they also acquired their
pottery. Although they were Piman speakers, the Areneños Pinacateños
had close cultural ties with the Yumans, remaining isolated from the
related Areneños and other Papago to the north and east. As mentioned
above, Hayden considers the Areneños Pinacateños to be descendants of
earlier Amargosans who migrated to the Sierra Pinacates. According
to Hayden, early cultural ties with the Yumans are apparent in the
appearance of Yuma I pottery in the Pinacates, placed at about A.D. 700
by Rogers. At this time there was very little contact with the Hohokam
culture and only some with the Trincheras culture. By Yuma II
(A.D. 1050-1500) and III (A.D. 1500-recent) times, it appears that
the Pinacateños had contact only with the Yumans.

Cultural remains associated with the Pinacateños include small
triangular concave base points, nodules of obsidian, scoria mortars,
figures in the desert pavement, and heaps of cremated game skeletons
similar to scattered calcined bone and sheep horn piles found elsewhere
in Areneños country. The Pinacate band was almost decimated by Mexican
military campaigns waged against them because of their attacks on
travelers using the El Camino del Diablo and by an 1851 epidemic. Their
last major camp, Sunset Camp south of the Pinacates, was abandoned by
1850. The remaining four or so families apparently settled among
other groups. With the possible exception of some Indians living
near Dome, Arizona (Vivian 1965), the Pinacateños are no longer
recognizable as a distinct group.

The Areneños of the second band also were primarily hunters and gatherers, although they did some farming in later times. They maintained contacts with Yumans and Papago, particularly the Papago Ho'oola (Huhura, Huhula) dialect group east of Ajo and in the Kaka district and south into Mexico (Fontana 1965: 100; Hayden 1967: 342, 1970: 87). The Areneños, who probably never numbered more than 100-150 (Hackenberg 1964: II-29), obtained their pottery from other Papago and may have made some of their own in later times. Their tools included bows and arrows, carrying nets; ceramic ollas, canteens, dippers, and cooking vessels; gourd water containers; digging sticks; baskets; harpooned fishing spears; manos and metates; mortars and pestles; stone projectile points, ceremonial paraphernalia, and a few musical instruments. They constructed circles of stacked rocks, which acted as windbreaks (Fontana 1964). In his combined description of both Areneños bands, Hackenberg listed their principal vegetal foods as camote, a root found in sand dunes; fruits of saguaro and pitahaya cacti; mesquite beans, and seeds of ironwood and chia. In addition to marine life, animal foods ranged from worms to mountain sheep, indicating that they ate just about anything (Hackenberg 1964: II-30). Lumholtz, an historic traveler through the region, listed three Sand Papago camp locations--Tinajas Altas, Tinajas de la Cabeza Prieta and Tinajas del Tule--all of which Hackenberg (1964: IV-20) interpreted as hunting camps.

Most historic accounts of the Areneños were from travelers using El Camino del Diablo, the only historic route that crossed through their territory, limiting our information to the southern portion of their range within southwestern Arizona. By the time of the Gadsden Purchase in 1854, there were no more accounts of Indians along El Camino del Diablo (Hackenberg 1964: IV-33). By this time the Areneños apparently had abandoned the areas and settled among other Papago at places like Sonoita and Santa Domingo in Sonora, and near Ajo and Quitobaquito in Arizona (Ezell 1954: 211; Hackenberg 1964: IV-38). The Hauhauwash dialect group, located near Menager Dam (Ali Ak Chin) in the southwest portion of the present-day Sells Papago Indian Reservation, claims descent from the Sand Papago (Hackenberg 1964: IV-85).

Spanish, Mexican and American

The following discussion of Spanish, Mexican and American activities in the central zone of the Papaguería is based on Hackenberg (1964), Fontana (1964) and Wagoner (1952). European activities to the west and east of the Papago Reservation have been summarized by McClellan and Vogler (1977) and by Betancourt (1978), respectively, and are not discussed here.

Spanish Period, 1540-1825

    Probably one of the first Spaniards to cross southwestern Arizona
was Melchior Diaz, who was connected with the Coronado expedition to the
north. In December, 1540, and January, 1541, Diaz traveled overland to and
from Sonora to California via what later came to be called El Camino del
Diablo. This route began in Sonoita, Sonora, passed Quitobaquito near
the present International Boundary, and circled a playa south of
the Sierra Pinta Mountains. From there the route passed through Tule
Tanks, south of the Cabeza Prieta Mountains, and tanks in the Tinajas
Altas Mountains before intersecting the Gila River not far from its
confluence with the Colorado River. El Camino del Diablo skirted most
of the central Papaguería, where the project area is found, and was the main
southern overland route to California prior to construction of the railroads.

    The European entrance of the central Papaguería occurred almost
a century and a half later. Father Eusebio Kino, a Jesuit missionary who
served in Pimería Alta between 1687 and 1711, and Juan Mateo Manje, a
Spanish soldier, are the first Europeans known to have visited central
Papaguería. Between 1690 and 1700 both Kino and Manje visited several
villages during their extensive travels through the Papago territory.
One of these settlements, Nuestra Senora de la Merced del Batki,
identified as the 19th century village of Batki (Kui Tatk), was within
8 miles of the present location of Sells (Haury 1950: 19).

    Between Kino's death in 1711 and the end of the Jesuit period in
1767, other military and religious reports confirmed the boundaries of
Papago territory described by Kino (Fontana 1964: 20). By the close of
the Jesuit period, Apache raiding had resulted in the Sobaipuri abandonment of the San Pedro Valley east of the Papaguería.

    In 1771 Garces, the first Franciscan superior for San Xavier
del Bac, journeyed from San Xavier to Sonoita and from there northwestward
along El Camino del Diablo to the Gila River, thereby skirting the central
zone of the Papaguería. In 1774 Garces and Father Juan Diaz accompanied
Juan Bautista de Anza from San Xavier to California and back. This
expedition took a similar route from San Xavier to the Gila River via
Sonoita, and returned along the Gila and Santa Cruz rivers. Although
the expedition did not cross the central zone itself, observations by
Anza on the reduction in the Papago population from smallpox and warfare
and on the replacement of mission Indians by Papagos born on the Papaguería
may indicate widespread demographic changes for this period.

    In 1775 Fathers Garces, Font and Eixarch accompanied the second
Anza expedition from San Xavier del Bac to California via the Gila and
Colorado rivers, and eventually returned overland by way of El Camino
del Diablo to Sonoita.

    In 1781 Pedro Fages led a military campaign from Sonoita to the
Yuma villages on the Colorado River. In October of that year, the

expedition crossed the Papaguería and encountered villages that Hackenberg (1964: IV-108) identifies as Komalik, Kui Tatk and Hickiwan. The fact that the expedition reported that inhabitants of an unnamed village north of Hickiwan were suffering from smallpox supports the hypothesis that the Spanish period was marked by demographic change. Hackenberg (1964) and Fontana (1964) report no expedition across the central Papaguería between 1781 and 1821, which marks the end of Spanish political control.

Spanish mining activities date from the 18th century discovery of silver in Guebavi, Sonora (1737), gold in Cienegilla, Sonora (1771), and the opening of mines in the Santa Cruz Valley (Fontana 1964: 43). The earliest mining in the central Papaguería centered in the Ajo Mountains, the Fresnal Canyon district on the west side of the Baboquivari Mountains, and the Cababi silver mines near the Comobabi Mountains; these mines probably date from the late 18th or early 19th century, since Americans found them littered with abandoned mining equipment in the mid-1800s (Hackenberg 1964: V-13).

At the turn of the century large cattle ranches were established in what had been Papago grasslands in the upper Sonoita, Santa Cruz and San Pedro drainages east of the central Papaguería (Wagoner 1952). Apparently, ranching was held in check by Apache raiding and did not expand into other grassland areas, such as the Baboquivari Valley. Wagoner mentions no ranches in central Papagueria prior to the American Civil War.

Mexican Period, 1825-1854

The second quarter of the 18th century witnessed an expansion of gold mining efforts near Quitovac, San Perfecto and La Basura in Mexico. The expansion into Papago territory resulted in conflict between Mexicans and Papagos. Hostilities soon escalated to a Western Papago revolt in 1840 and culminated in the intervention of Mexican federal troups in 1843.

During the Mexican period, mineral extraction continued in the Ajo, Baboquivari and Comobabi mountains of the central Papaguería. U.S. military reports from the mid-19th century indicate that Mexican and Papago settlements were in close proximity in the Fresnal Canyon district. To what extent this was due to the exigencies of very limited water resources or reflects economic and/or social ties between Mexicans and Papagos is not clear.

In his discussion of mining in Pima County, Hinton (1970: 122-24) attests to the antiquity of mining in the Ajo, Baboquivari, Comobabi, Quijotoa and Santa Rosa mountains, and attributes several settlements in these districts to Mexicans. Although the Mexican War ceased in 1848, the central Papaguería did not come under the jurisdiction of the United States until the completion of the Gadsden Purchase in 1854.

American Period, 1855-1931

Although most followed the Gila River, a few explorations and military expeditions did cross the central Papaguería. John W. Audobon, a "forty-niner," first crossed the central Papaguería on a south to north journey from Altar to the Pima-Maricopa villages on the Gila River in 1849.

In May, 1854, Colonel A.B. Gray traversed central Papaguería while surveying a route for the Southern Pacific Railroad. He reported that the Ajo mines were reopened in 1854 by a San Francisco mining company, employing Papago labor.

Charles D. Poston, manager of the Enriquetta Mine near Tubac and later Superintendent of Indian Affairs for Arizona Territory, also visited the Ajo mines while on an exploratory mission into the Gadsden Purchase in 1854-1855.

In 1855 the Boundary Commission, led by W.H. Emory, surveyed and marked the United States-Mexican boundary of the Gadsden Purchase. They passed through the Baboquivari Mountains, where they found Papagos raising cattle and horses, and then traveled westward to Sonoita.

In 1858 the Ehrenberg Map was published; this document, based on mining explorations by Ehrenberg, Major Heintzelman, Lieutenant Parks and others, shows gold placer mines at Ajo, Quijotoa, Sonoita and Quitovac, as well as several claims in the Santa Cruz Valley. Fresnal and Cababi were not recorded on this map, perhaps an indication that they were not known at this date.

Civil War correspondence cited by Hackenberg (1964: IV-123) also is relevant to mining in the Comobabi and Baboquivari mountains north and east of the project area. Major Coult, in a letter dated October 2, 1862, reported two mines at Fresnal. On April 14, 1863, Colonel Ferguson reported 27 Mexican families at Fresnal, an additional mine (La Mina Prieta) 4.5 miles to the south, and a mine worked by nine Mexicans at Cababi (Comobabi Mountains). Pumpelly and Poston, forced to retreat from the latter's mining operations near Tubac, passed through the Baboquivari Valley in 1861. They recorded abandoned mines and a Papago village at Fresnal, a cattle and horse ranch at Pozo Verde, and a Mexican mine and Papago village at Cababi during their retreat.

With the end of Apache raids in the 1870s Anglo mining on the Papaguería increased rapidly, as documented by Hinton (1970), Clotts (1915) and Bryan (1925). After being briefly restricted in the 1930s, non-Indian mining entry was closed in 1955 (Fontana 1964: 48).

Like mining, stock raising on the Papaguería did not reach a peak until after 1875, although it began much earlier. Hackenberg (1964: V-11) states that in areas such as southeastern Papaguería, where grass was more abundant, cattle and horses have played a limited

role in Papago subsistence since the Spanish period; he documents
the presence of domestic stock at Fresnal Canyon, Pan Tak and Pozo
Verde in the Baboquivari Valley in 1855 and 1861 (Hackenberg 1964:
IV,123-24). Limited cattle production for local Anglo consumption
began in the Papaguería shortly after the close of the Civil War.
During the 1860s Thomas Childs brought a herd of 200 head into the
Ajo Mountains and in 1869 Colonel Hooker leased Papago rangeland in
the Baboquivari Valley for 4,000 head of cattle, before permanently
settling near Willcox, Arizona.

Stock production for the national market was begun by both
Anglos and Papagos after the completion of the Southern Pacific Railroad
in 1882. The Papago villages of San Miguel, Chukut Kuk, Topawa and
Vamori, in the Vamori drainage south of Sells, were involved in
stock production by the turn of the century.

By the 1890s drought and arroyo cutting resulted in the drastic
deterioration of rangeland throughout southern Arizona, and Anglo
encroachment on traditional Papago territory brought Anglos and
Papagos into direct competition for the diminishing grasslands. The
Anglo threat to the Papago cattle industry became so serious that Papagos
began "appropriating" non-Indian cattle at this time. The Sells Indian
Reservation, established in 1916 on the basis of a survey of Papago
land use and occupancy by Clotts and Engle (Clotts 1915), was set aside
in part to minimize the Anglo threat to Papago ranching. Anglo ranching
effectively ended in 1931, when the present boundaries of the Papago
Indian Reservation were established.

Before concluding this chapter, it is necessary to briefly
outline the history of the town of Sells. The settlement of Artesa
first appeared on the 1909 Government Land Office map in the present
location of Sells (Granger 1960: 281). By 1915 two settlements,
Indian Oasis and Artesa, were reported at the north end of the Artesa
Mountains (Clotts 1915: 35, 59-60). Indian Oasis, so called because it
was the only place with a permanent well, was described by Clotts (1915:
59-60) as follows:

[Indian Oasis, Township 7 South, Range 4 East, Section 25] is
the center of travel to all parts of Papaguería, including
Sonora, Mexico. There is a large store owned by Joseph
Menanger, who enjoys a large trade from nearly all the
southern part of the country. He has dug two wells....
He has a large ranch of 71 acres upon which he raises
...wheat, barley, peas, etc., by means of an irrigation
ditch about a mile long which takes storm water from an
arroyo.

There is an Indian farmer..., and family, an Indian Service
physician...and family, a Presbyterian missionary,...and
family. The latter [has] built a church, used also as a
school,...and dug a well....

Mr. John Tierney (white) has a homestead of 140 acres
and a house here, and is digging a well.

A Government school site has been selected here and the
Indian Service is now drilling a well here to supply
the school, the farmer and the physician.

There are in all 15 white people, 7 Mexicans, 20 Yaki
Indians and 44 Papagos here. [The latter were in Artesa.]

There are in all 378 acres of fields here of which 133 are
Papago fields.

Clotts (1915: 35) locates Artesa in Sections 19 and 30, Township 17
South, Range 5 East, which would be about one mile northwest of the
location shown on the 1948 United States Geological Survey (U.S.G.S.),
Sells 15 minute Quadrangle. This discrepancy may be due to differences
between the Land Office survey and the Aspass allotment survey used by
Clotts as a base map (Clotts 1915: 15, 60). Clotts (1915: 35)
described Artesa as follows:

[Artesa] is the Indian part of Indian Oasis. There are 12
houses near the wells and 8 near the charco 2 miles east of the
wells. They have a population of 44. There is a store owned
by Mariana Johnson, who is also Indian Policemen. They have
two wells,...with plenty of water at all times. There is a
corral at the wells and one at the charco. The charco is one
of the largest and best, is fenced and has a U.S.I.S. trough
installed. They have 133 acres of fields near here.

In 1918 Indian Oasis was renamed Sells, in honor of Cato Sells,
then commissioner of Indian Affairs (Granger 1960: 281). With the
construction of the Sells Agency headquarters, Sells assumed an
important administrative role on the newly created Sells Indian
Reservation. Today, the village of Sells continues to grow in size
and importance as a major political and service center on the Reservation.

Summary

The preceramic period is poorly documented, both in the project
area and in the central zone of the Papagueria as a whole. Preceramic
occupations occur in the Quijotoa Valley 40 miles west of the project
area and at Ventana Cave 40 miles northwest of the project area but
only isolated preceramic materials have been recorded in the project area.

The ceramic period (Hohokam) occupation is better known, both
within the project area and within the central zone of the Papagueria.
The project area is within the region occupied in prehistoric times by
the Desert Hohokam, who may initially have been colonists from the
Gila-Salt Basin. By the Sells phase, these groups were settled in
small dispersed villages and practiced a mixed economy of gathering,

hunting and agriculture; wild foodstuffs probably dominated the prehistoric diet. Desert Hohokam groups had ties with other regions, as evidenced by the presence of shell from coastal regions, non-indigenous pottery and other trade items. Red-on-buff and red-on-brown decorated wares, polished redwares and trincheras pottery show relationships with the Gila-Salt Basin, the Tucson Basin and Sonora, Mexico. Small quantities of Lower Colorado buffware indicate some ties with that area also, but these relationships appear to be stronger in the valleys west of the project area. Much remains to be learned about the nature of these regional relationships. Major changes in settlement and subsistence practices and in material culture occur in the Classic period, both within the central Papaguería and in surrounding regions. In the former, change is marked by an apparent increase in the number of settlements and in the appearance of trincheras features and the possible selection of easily defensible sites for village locations. In the Tucson Basin and the Gila-Salt Basin, this period is marked by the appearance of Saladoan traits and ends with the abandonment of the large riverine villages.

The period between A.D. 1450 and 1700 is not well understood in the project area or elsewhere in the Sonoran Desert. At the time of contact, Piman-speaking groups were found in areas prehistorically occupied by the River and Desert Hohokam. A direct link between the Hohokam and the Piman groups, though likely, has not been proved. Comparatively few sites of this critical period have been located and fewer still have been studied in detail. Sites from this period have been reported in the project area, and further investigations there may shed light on the problem of continuity between the Hohokam and Piman groups.

The area immediately west of Sells appears to have been a focus of Papago occupation since the early contact period. Occupied from at least the late 17th century to the mid-19th century, Batki (Kui Tatk) and its related fields at Gu Oidak are less than 12 miles from Sells; like Sells, they are on tributaries of Vamori Wash. In view of the proximity of a long-term historic Papago occupation of Sells, it is not surprising that an historic camp dating around A.D. 1700 ± 100 has been discovered in the project area.

The town of Sells, the most recent occupation of the project area, dates from the early 20th century. Soon after the establishment of the Sells Reservation, Sells became a major service center for the reservation, a role it continues to play today.

From the above discussion and from data presented in Chapter 5, it is evident that the project area and surrounding territory have witnessed human occupation, with few gaps, probably from the Vamori phase and certainly from the Sells phase of the Desert Hohokam sequence to the present day. Such a long sequence of occupation indicates that important problems in Desert Hohokam, post-Classic and Contact period archaeology can be addressed in the project area. Prehistoric, as well as historic cultural resources, in the project area may be of cultural or ethnic significance to the present residents of Sells, in view of the likelihood of a Hohokam-Piman link.

CHAPTER 5

SUMMARY AND EVALUATION OF PREVIOUS RESEARCH IN THE CENTRAL PAPAGUERÍA

The following summary and evaluation of previous archaeological research is first divided into sections on the project area and the central Papaguería. Within each section are three main periods of research: the pre-1945 studies, studies between 1945 and 1970 and studies after 1970. This summary is offered as a means of identifying inadequacies in current knowledge and as a basis for defining a set of appropriate problems for future archaeological research in the project area.

Project Area

As described in Chapter 2, the project area is an irregular parcel approximately 12.75 square miles in area surrounding Sells, Arizona, and incorporating the Sells Wash flood plain and the northern extension of the Artesa Mountains. Only portions of this parcel have been examined for archaeological resources, and, as a result, only a partial inventory of cultural resources has been completed. Previous research does, however, provide a knowledge of the range of archaeological materials likely to be found in the project area.

Archaeological research in the project area spans most of the 20th century, but can be divided into two major periods of work: the pre-World War II era and the post-1970 period. Little research was done in the interim. Pre-World War II efforts generally were broad regional studies of the Papaguería. Surveys that entered the project area include Huntington (1914), Gila Pueblo, and the Arizona State Museum/Department of Anthropology. In the 1970s, work in the project area is characterized by a focus on more limited problems or on more limited areas. These studies include dissertation research by Stacy (1974) and small scale contract projects by the National Park Service and the Arizona State Museum. These three eras of research are summarized separately below.

Research Prior to 1945

Huntington (1914), a geographer interested in the problem of climate change and its effect on the southwestern landscape, described walled sites on a series of hills northwest of Sells in the vicinity of Etoi Ki. A portion of the isolated volcanic outcrop on which these sites are found falls within the project boundaries.

The first strictly archaeological research recorded in the project area consisted of reconnaissance by Gila Pueblo in 1928 and 1929. At that

time the research goals of this institution were to define the areal extent
of the "Red-on-buff culture" (now known as the Hohokam) in the lower and
middle Gila Basin and in the Papaguería, and to determine its origin
(Gladwin and Gladwin 1929 a, b; 1930). Because of the vast territory
to be covered and the nature of the research problem, ground inspections
apparently were confined to easily accessible locations where sites were
expected, such as flood plains adjacent to washes, stream confluences,
or permanent water sources. Because of the focus on "red-on-buff" sites,
data are biased toward later and more "visible" archaeological manifestations, particularly large, dense sherd and lithic scatters with
trash mounds. Small scatters, preceramic or nonceramic scatters, and
limited activity areas tend to be under-represented in the Gila Pueblo
survey. Gila Pueblo personnel did not document areas in which they
found no archaeological materials so that their data are inadequate
for predicting site locations. Additional problems with using Gila
Pueblo site information for planning purposes stem from the fact that
U.S.G.S. 7.5 minute and 15 minute scale topographic maps were lacking
for the Papaguería at the time of the survey, and precise site locations
could not be plotted. With few exceptions, descriptions of locations,
directions to sites and map locations shown in Gladwin and Gladwin
(1929b) are far too general to reconstruct the precise location without
costly resurvey.

According to the Gladwins (Gladwin and Gladwin 1929b), sites in
the Baboquivari Valley typically were small and inconspicuous; some
occurred without surface features, while others contained small trash
mounds. They noted that with the exception of sites on the Santa Cruz
River and near Sells, trash mounds were uncommon and never large (Gladwin
and Gladwin 1929b: 117). According to site forms on file at the Arizona
State Museum, two sites near the Sells project area exhibit the unusual
features of a "stadium-shaped mound" and a "Sun Temple-like mound"
(possibly a reservoir). They did not speculate on the function of such
features, other than to note that some are found in areas suitable for
drainage reception (Gladwin and Gladwin 1929b: 118).

The Gila Pueblo archaeologists also knew of trincheras structures
in the Baboquivari Valley and observed that they were characterized by
few sherds, numerous bedrock mortars, and few pictographs. Like later
workers in the area, they found that sherd areas and mounds were located
in the plains (valley floors) suitable for agriculture, in contrast to
rock shelters and trincheras sites, which occurred in the mountains.

Frank Midvale (Mitalsky), an archaeologist for Gila Pueblo,
recorded 11 sites in the Sells 15 minute Quadrangle; two sites
appear to have been assigned duplicate field numbers and a third is
most likely in the Vamori Quadrangle to the south. Of the eight remaining Gila Pueblo sites, three appear to be in the project area.
These are: G.P. (Gila Pueblo) Sonora D:1:1, a lithic scatter; G.P.
Sonora D:1:7/8, a village with at least four trash mounds, and
G.P. Sonora D:1:6, a small settlement with a single trash mound.

G.P. Sonora D:1:2, recorded as a small village with two trash mounds and
"5 or 6 stony spots" 2 miles east of Sells (1928 boundaries), probably
is within the project limits.

Between 1938 and the early years of World War II, the Arizona
State Museum and the Department of Anthropology of the University of
Arizona undertook a series of archaeological and ethnological studies
in the Papaguería. The archaeological studies, coordinated by Emil
W. Haury, included reconnaissance surveys throughout central Papaguería
and excavations at Valshni Village (Scantling 1940), Jackrabbit Ruin
(Withers 1941), and Ventana Cave (Haury 1950). Additional studies at Ash
Hill have not been published. These investigations were aimed at the development of a regional chronology for the Papaguería. Since the excavations are
outside the project boundaries, they are discussed in greater detail
in the section on the central Papaguería; the following discussion is
addressed to survey efforts in the vicinity of Sells.

Between 1938 and 1940 Alden W. Jones, an employee of the U.S.I.S.
(United States Indian Service) Roads Office living in Sells, led Haury
and students to sites he had identified in the vicinity; 25 sites in the
ASM survey files for the Sells Quadrangle were identified as a part
of this reconnaissance. Approximately one-half of the recorded sites
are south of Sells in the Vamori and Valshni drainages; 11 are in the
Sells drainage, and three of these are in the project area. These include
AZ DD:1:10, a Papago sherd scatter at least 100 years old; AZ DD:1:22,
a Sells phase village; and AZ DD:1:25, a dense scatter with possible
dates between A.D. 1450 and 1750.

Although precise locations have been plotted for these sites, the
early ASM survey data are also difficult to use for planning purposes.
The survey efforts were not directed toward obtaining a complete inventory of cultural resources, but rather toward locating sites suitable
for excavation, such as ceramic period stratified sites that could answer
questions about chronology and culture history. Thus a bias toward
later dense scatters with trash mounds and against the smaller sites is
present in the sample. Survey coverage was uneven and generally was
confined to locations where sites were expected or to sites previously
identified by local inhabitants. Finally, there is no record of surveyed
areas in which sites were not found. Thus it is not known whether
the lower number of recorded sites along Sells Wash (as compared with
Vamori Wash) reflects differential survey coverage, differential depositional
effects, or less intensive occupation in the prehistoric past.

By the end of the 1930s certain key facts were known about prehistoric sites in the vicinity of Sells. Extensive lithic scatters,
small sherd and lithic scatters from the ceramic period, large valley
floor sites with trash mounds, and cerros de trincheras sites in the mountains had been recorded. At least one possible protohistoric site also
had been identified. Together, these resources indicated that the Sells
area had a long and varied history of occupation. Further, they suggested
that the region was suitable for the investigation of at least two
critical problems in Papaguería prehistory: 1) the cultural affiliation

and function of cerros de trincheras sites, and 2) the problem of continuity between the Hohokam and Piman speakers. Excavated sites just outside the project area aided the development of a regional chronology.

There were deficiencies in the early research and many important questions remained to be answered. As noted above, survey was not systematic, so that the site inventory was incomplete and biased. Information recorded on site survey cards was sketchy and data on features and lithic assemblages, site locations and detailed maps usually were lacking. Most important, there was little understanding of how the sites functioned together as part of a regional system, and ties between the Papagueria and other areas were ill defined. While hypotheses about the relationship between sites in the Salt-Gila Basin and the Papagueria had been offered (Haury 1950), these were not fully tested; nothing was known of possible relationships with areas in Mexico.

Research Between 1945 and 1970

The period between World War II and the 1970s saw little archaeological work in the project area. After survey by Haury and his students, no additional prehistoric sites were recorded in the project area until 1962, when Cipriano Manuel, then the Papago tribal judge, reported the discovery of a buried prehistoric (Sells phase?) village with recent Papago trash. The site, which is adjacent to Sells Wash, is recorded in ASM site survey files as AZ DD:1:29.

Research in the 1970s

During the 1970s survey efforts in the project area were renewed and excavations were initiated. These efforts, discussed in detail below, include 1) an examination of cerros de trincheras sites and adjacent scatters (Stacy 1974), 2) survey and limited testing for the Sells-Gu Oidak road by the National Park Service, and 3) limited studies for various construction projects within Sells by the National Park Service and the Arizona State Museum. Surveyed areas within the project area are shown in Figure 2. With the exception of Stacy's research and a brief housing survey by Doelle and Brew (1976), these investigations have not been reported.

As the basis of her doctoral dissertation for the Department of Anthropology, University of Arizona, Stacy (1974) examined five of the seven previously recorded cerros de trincheras in the Baboquivari Valley and recorded additional sites at the bases of the trincheras sites. In the Sells area, Stacy studied sites in and near the topographic features called Etoi Ki and Suwuk Tontk on the 1948 Sells 15 minute Quadrangle. At each site data on features, types of artifacts and kinds of raw materials used for lithic manufacture were recorded in order to define the kinds of activities represented in the archaeological

record. On the basis of ceramic data, Stacy indicated that the sites were
occupied during the Sells phase (A.D. 1200-1400), and identified general
differences between hill and valley floor assemblages in the Baboquivari
Valley.

Stacy concluded (1974: 190-93) that the hill sites and the sites
below them represent two different activity configurations, based on a
comparison of features and artifacts. Hill sites showed evidence of
1) primary reduction of cryptocrystalline stone; 2) food processing
in bedrock mortars; 3) habitation or shelter in circular structures; and
4) activities involving Sells Plain containers. Manos, hearths and
ashy deposits indicative of long term deposition usually are absent.
Distinct activities are inferred from the presence of rockwork
structures that do not appear at the valley floor sites.

Stacy indicated that the following activities occurred on the
valley sites: 1) primary and secondary flaking; 2) food processing with
manos and metates; 3) use of mescal knives; 4) use of hearths; 5) use
of ceramic containers, including Sells Red bowls; 6) manufacture and
processing with scrapers of igneous material; 7) trash disposal in
mounds; and 8) longer term habitation as indicated by ashy soil and
greater artifact density and site size. While the observations regarding
rockwork, artifact density, deposition and site size appear to
be valid, the differences between hill and valley artifact assemblages
are less clear cut than Stacy indicates. An examination of her Table 24
(Stacy 1974: 164) shows that, with the exception of the large village of
AZ DD:1:2, hill and valley sites have rather similar artifact assemblages.
One can draw two different conclusions on the basis of this evidence.
Either a similar range of activities is represented at hill and valley
sites, or the presence or absence of broad categories of artifacts is
not a sufficiently sensitive measure of the differences between these
sites. At this point, the small sample of sites, the great variability
in sites below the hills and the lack of excavation data make the
function of trincheras sites a matter of speculation. In recognition
of the tentative nature of her findings, Stacy posed several hypotheses
for activities specific to hill sites. Testing these hypotheses was beyond
the scope of her research but her subjective impression was that
cerros de trincheras served as defensive sites and/or provided micro-
climates suitable for growing small or specialized crops.

Suwuk Tontk and Etoi Ki, two settlement complexes studied by
Stacy, border on the project area on the south and northwest. Immediately
north of the previously recorded Suwuk Tontk site (AZ DD:1:1) are a lithic
scatter (AZ DD:1:41) and two sherd and lithic scatters with a predominance of chipped stone (AZ DD:1:38 and AZ DD:1:39); Stacy identified
these as quarries (ASM site survey files). South of AZ DD:1:1 is a sherd
and lithic scatter (AZ DD:1:40) of an unidentified function; an additional
quarry (AZ DD:1:32) was recorded by Stacy northwest of AZ DD:1:1, but it
was not discussed in her dissertation.

The second complex of sites near Etoi Ki contains two trincheras
sites (AZ DD:1:3 and AZ DD:1:5), which Stacy restudied. In addition
to these, Stacy recorded five valley floor sites (AZ DD:1:33-37) at the
base of Etoi Ki. These range from sparse sherd scatters (AZ DD:1:36
and AZ DD:1:37) and small villages (AZ DD:1:33 and AZ DD:1:35) to
large villages with a variety of features, such as trash mounds, artifact concentrations, lithic activity areas, hearths, petroglyphs and
bedrock mortars (AZ DD:1:2 and AZ DD:1:34). AZ DD:1:33, a Sells phase
village with two trash mounds, and AZ DD:1:34, a large Sells phase
village with numerous features, extend into the project area.

Stacy's research made several important contributions to Papaguería
prehistory. First, Stacy attempted to treat spatially related sites
as part of a settlement-subsistence system, rather than as isolated
phenomena, as had previously been done. Second, she provided detailed
data on whole artifact assemblages rather than on ceramics alone, with the
result that her site information is more complete than earlier records.
Third, she attempted to characterize the function of cerros de trincheras
sites on the basis of artifactual data, rather than on the basis of location alone, thereby putting interpretations of site functions on a
much sounder footing. Finally, she offered a concise summary of documented 19th century Papago settlement and subsistence patterns, and
extrapolated these into the prehistoric past based on similarities in
historic and prehistoric (Sells phase) site locations. The latter
contribution is of particular significance because it implies that
data on 19th century settlement patterns can be used to more accurately
predict locations of specific kinds of prehistoric sites.

Since 1973 the National Park Service and the Arizona State Museum
have undertaken limited contract studies in the Sells area. As part of
an extended federal program of road construction and improvement on the
Papago Reservation, the Western Archeological Center, National Park Service, surveyed Papago Indian Road (PIR) 24, the road from Sells to
Gu Oidak. Stacy (1973: 11-12) reports that in June 1973 Papago archaeology trainees recorded three sherd and lithic scatters (PIR 119, 120,
121) between one and two miles west of Sells, an unspecified number of
small plainware scatters of fewer than 20 sherds, and a few isolated
artifacts. The exact site locations and more detailed data are lacking,
since Stacy was unable to visit these sites.

In November, 1973, a crew supervised by John Clonts (WAC) resurveyed PIR 24 and identified 30 archaeological loci. A review of the
unpublished field forms, maps and testing notes on file at WAC provided
the following data. Ten of the 30 archaeological loci were combined into
two sites, yielding a total of 19 artifact concentrations and three
occurrences of isolated artifacts or recent features. Ten of the concentrations were given ASM site numbers and six of these features were
tested for subsurface deposits or features, with negative results. At
least three scatters, PIR 3 and 4 and AZ DD:1:42, were found in areas
disturbed by dike construction. Inspections of the disturbed area

indicate that cultural materials may be buried under as much as 30 cm of soil. The brief descriptions available characterized most sites as sparse surface scatters without discernible features in the right-of-way, but because portions of the sites outside the 100-foot-wide right-of-way were not inspected, information on these sites is incomplete. With the exception of one site with red-on-buff ceramics, all of the sites were characterized by brownwares that were not identified in the field. The artifacts collected have not been analyzed; consequently, the temporal and cultural affiliation of these scatters is uncertain.

Four scatters (PIR 3, PIR 4, AZ DD:1:42 and AZ DD:1:45) are in the project area. One isolated artifact (PIR 9), an isolated mano and a fire pit (PIR 8), and 11 additional artifact scatters (PIR 11, PIR 17, PIR 23 and AZ DD:1:43, 44 and 46-51) were found in the area between the project boundaries and the well fields. The remaining four scatters (PIR 13-16) and two isolated artifacts (PIR 12) recorded on the survey lie west of the well fields. According to Stacy, the area one to two miles west of Sells is subject to alluviation (Stacy 1973: 11); this suggests that the Sells Wash area is suitable for akchin farming and increases the likelihood of buried prehistoric remains in this setting.

In November 1974 Douglas Brown (WAC), inspected a 900 foot (east-west) by 800 foot (north-south) portion of the old Sells Rodeo Arena where construction of the Tribal Office Building Complex was planned (see Figure 2). He discovered two sparse sherd and lithic scatters (Rodeo 1 and 2) in disturbed areas between the arena and Sells Wash. Rodeo 1 is a 10 m diameter scatter of thin, red, polished plainware sherds and a few flakes. Rodeo 2 consists of flakes, cores and a few brownware sherds scattered over an area 20 m in diameter. No evidence of features or deposition was found at either site. No cultural or temporal affiliation was assigned to either scatter. Since construction was planned to avoid the scatters, further data recovery was not required.

In March, 1976, Brown and other Park Service archaeologists visited an area below Etoi Ki where construction of a livestock pavilion and new rodeo ground was underway (D. Brown 1976). They recorded mortars, trincheras-like architecture, petroglyphs, scattered sherds and lithics, and an abundance of soft red stone. They estimated that the site ended just south of the new rodeo grounds. Brown later discovered that they had inspected AZ DD:1:34, a site previously recorded by Stacy, who reported that the boundaries extended to the Sells-Ajo road (Route 86). If Stacy's observation is correct, then rodeo construction did affect a portion of the site.

On October 26 and 27, 1976, William H. Doelle and Susan A. Brew, of the Cultural Resource Management Section of the Arizona State Museum, surveyed various parcels of land in Sells for a proposed pre-school, a proposed health services complex and 104 proposed housing units. Doelle

and Brew found no archaeological resources in the disturbed parcel for
the proposed preschool, but did record one site, AZ DD:1:21, at the
proposed location for the health services complex. This site was
described in a letter report (Teague 1976: 1, 2) as a reasonably well
preserved sherd and lithic surface scatter that may date to the protohistoric or early historic periods. Two possible site functions,
agriculture and food gathering and processing, were proposed for
further investigations. It was believed at the time that the reworked
base of a late Archaic point and the possible Archaic point tip were
re-used by later peoples, but this assumption also required further
testing. Data recovery was recommended to mitigate the impact of the
proposed construction on the site.

The following information on survey coverage of the housing lots
is based on a conversation with Susan A. Brew in 1978 and a survey
report by Doelle and Brew (1976). Brew stated that the subdivision survey
was bounded by Route 86 on the north, the foothills on the east, a dirt
road exten ion of Main Street on the south and a road on the west side
of Lots 74, 75 and 76 on the west. Within this parcel, undisturbed
areas were intensively surveyed, the areas around existing houses were
casually inspected and fenced lots were not examined. No survey was
done in the two "extensions" south of the main subdivision area where
drainage and water control work will be done. The subdivision contained
prehistoric and recent historic cultural material, but none of sufficient
density or integrity to be accorded site status. In addition to the
subdivision parcel, 28 isolated lots also were surveyed. The locations
of scme lots are in question, since the Phoenix Western Engineers, Inc.
base map does not correspond exactly to the base map supplied by STRAAM
Engineers, Inc., which was drafted from aerial photographs. Brew is of
the opinion that the locations of the isolated lots were inexact. Other
parcels shown on current Papago Housing Authority and Tribal Utilities
maps were added after the survey by Doelle and Brew and have not been
surveyed. Appendices B and C summarize the discrepancies between lots shown
on the two base maps and lists lots not surveyed by Doelle and Brew.
Doelle and Brew (1976) reported that the isolated lots contained few
cultural remains. Where present, these materials were too sparse or too
disturbed to warrant site status.

In September 1977, Nancy T. Curriden and Carolyn Carter (ASM)
completed data recovery from AZ DD:1:21, the site recorded by Doelle
and Brew and reported by Teague (1976). The data recovery operations
were summarized in an unpublished report by Curriden (n.d.b). Surface
materials were collected from 231 5 m by 5 m grids. These covered the
entire portion of the site within the health services complex, as
well as a southeastern extension of the site not seen on the survey. In
order to determine whether subsurface cultural materials were present,
Curriden and Carter excavated test pits, ranging in size from 1 m by
1 m to 1.5 m by 1.5 m, in five areas of greater artifact density. Three
of the pits were devoid of subsurface materials. The remaining two
revealed an ash and charcoal layer ranging in depth from 6 cm to 20 cm
below the surface and an eroded cluster of rocks with flecks of charcoal
1 cm to 2 cm below the surface.

Curriden's brief report focused on questions of site activities and cultural and temporal affiliation. Ceramics were classified into existing typological categories in order to determine the date of occupation of the site. The most abundant sherds were protohistoric plainwares predating 1860, followed by historic Papago plainwares post-dating 1860. A few sherds transitional between Santa Cruz and Sacaton Red-on-buff, Sells Red and a mica-tempered plainware with and without interior smudging also were recovered. Curriden attributes the recent Papago sherds to recent post-occupational disturbance, a view supported by the absence of pre-World War I Anglo goods and the presence of recent glass bottles, plastic containers and metal stirrups (Curriden n.d.b: 9, 10). On the basis of ceramic identifications by Bruce Masse, she assigned the protohistoric date of A.D. 1700 ± 100 to the surface scatter. Because the sherds averaged only 2.5 cm in diameter, Curriden did not attempt to determine vessel shape and size.

Lithic materials were analyzed with the goal of determining the cultural-temporal affiliation and range of activities represented by the scatter. The assemblage consisted of cores, flake cores, decortication flakes and shatter, and a small number (7.5 percent) of formal tools, of which few were diagnostic. Flakes were further subdivided into categories based on the amount and location of cortex, in order to assess tool production stages represented at the site. No microwear analyses were performed; however, the unifacial retouch visible without a microscope suggested that tools were used for scraping rather than cutting motions. Curriden (n.d.b: 13) saw no strong patterning in the artifact distribution, although some clustering of materials was evident; she suggests that from one to three possible areas of core reduction may have been present, but have been obscured by erosion. The few diagnostic items ranged from late Archaic to protohistoric periods, but the earlier tools showed evidence of reworking, an indication that a later date for the site is appropriate. On the basis of the artifact inventory, Curriden interprets the scatter as a campsite where core reduction, limited tool use and limited plant processing occurred, probably during the protohistoric period.

Curriden's report suffers somewhat from brevity, but is otherwise methodologically sound. Because the raw data on which her interpretations are based have not yet been incorporated in the manuscript, her conclusions cannot be fully evaluated; however, they appear to be reasonable. The investigation at this site is significant, in that (1) it provides evidence for the protohistoric use of the Sells vicinity, an area not specifically mentioned in the historic documents; (2) it is the only well described excavation in the project area; and (3) it demonstrated that even somewhat disturbed surface scatters can provide information on site activities.

As a group, the contract projects provide documentation for small sites overlooked by earlier studies and confirm previous observations that the Sells vicinity witnessed extensive occupation during the late protohistoric periods. Both the frequency of isolated remains noted by

Doelle and Brew and by Clonts, and the frequent occurrence of small
sherd scatters along the Gu Oidak-Sells road certainly point to a
greater site density than was previously indicated by less systematic
surveys. It is important to note that virtually every contract
survey in the project area has yielded evidence of a prehistoric or
historic occupation, and it is likely that many unrecorded sites also
exist.

The chief deficiency of the contract work is, of course, the
lack of published data. As a consequence, recent studies, other than
Stacy's investigations, have added little of substance to prehistory
of the Sells Basin or of the Papaguería as a whole.

Central Papaguería

Research Prior to 1945

Two of the three most important studies in Papaguería prehistory were undertaken within 15 miles of Sells between 1938 and 1940.
Excavations at Jackrabbit Ruin (Scantling 1940) and Valshni Village
(Withers 1941) were complementary efforts that resulted in the development
of a regional chronology for the prehistoric period. Together these
studies form the baseline against which other excavations are compared.
The discussion of these two pioneer investigations deals first with
methods and findings at each site, and concludes with an evaluation of
the significance and deficiencies of the research.

The last of these three projects was the excavation of Ventana
Cave some 40 air miles northwest of Sells. This project, under the
direction of Emil W. Haury, was supervised in the field by Wilfred C.
Bailey in spring of 1941 and by Julian D. Hayden in spring of 1942.
The stratified deposits of the cave provided a record of human
occupation from the late Pleistocene to the very recent past and formed
the basis for our understanding of the past culture history of the
Papaguería. The evaluation of the Ventana Cave project, excerpted in part
from McClellan and Vogler (1977), follows the discussion of Scantling's
and Withers' excavations.

Frederick H. Scantling and a Papago CCC-ID labor crew excavated
Jackrabbit Ruin (AZ DD:1:6) between November 15, 1938, and April 15,
1939; the results were published in 1940 as Scantling's master's thesis
for the Department of Anthropology, University of Arizona. Because
"surface indications seemed typical for the region and evidences of
occupation were extensive" (Scantling 1940: 2), Jackrabbit Ruin was selected for
excavation in the hopes of establishing a sequence of phases for the
Papaguería based on changing culture traits. Scantling discovered through
excavation that the site represented a single phase corresponding to no
known Hohokam phase. Scantling named this the Sells phase, and defined

it as the co-occurrence of Sells Red, Sells Plain and Tanque Verde Red-on-brown ceramics. He dated the Sells phase to the period between A.D. 1200 and 1400 on the basis of the occurrence of Gila Polychrome with Sells Red and Tanque Verde Red-on-brown (Scantling 1940: 35).

At the start of field work, the entire site covering an area of 90,000 m^2 was resurveyed and 78 features comprised of numerous sherd concentrations and some 30 trash mounds were marked with stakes and mapped. The largest of the mounds, which ranged from 0.3 m to 2.0 m in height and from 8 m to 25 m in diameter, was selected for the first test excavation.

Since the methods used to excavate the mounds at Jackrabbit Ruin and Valshni Village were quite similar, the procedures employed at Jackrabbit Ruin will be outlined briefly. A 1 m wide trench was dug along the north-south axis of Mound 33 and artifacts observed during excavation were collected. After the transect was completed to sterile soil, the adjacent 1 m wide strip was removed as a "stratitest" (Withers 1941: 2). For this, the strip was divided into 1 m by 1 m grids and excavated in arbitrary 50 cm levels; all dirt was screened. Sherd counts from each 1 m by 1 m by 0.5 m block were then compared for changes through time.

During the excavation of the initial trench in Mound 33, it became apparent that two walls of an adobe enclosure had been cut through; therefore, after the stratitest was completed, the exterior walls of the enclosure were defined and the interior trash deposits were removed. Scantling does not mention what excavation units were used, so it is not known whether the trash was removed as a single 2.5 m thick unit, as several arbitrary levels or by natural stratigraphy. No prepared floor or floor features were discovered and Scantling (1940: 20) stated that it was not possible to assign a function to this adobe enclosure.

A second stratigraphic test was placed in Mound 48, using similar techniques, although no initial trench was dug. No profiles or discussion of stratigraphy of this mound were offered, but Scantling noted that Mounds 48 and 33 were quite similar.

Controlled testing also was undertaken in Compound B, a 47 m by 48 m area situated 0.5 m higher than the surrounding ground level and enclosed on four sides by an earthen ridge. This enclosed space was divided into quadrants by two trenches; each quadrant was then divided into 1 m by 2 m grids and alternating grids were excavated to sterile soil in order to expose features. Several house floors, outdoor hearths and roasting pits were located in Compound B, but detailed descriptions of these features are lacking.

Outside Compound B and Mounds 33 and 48 Scantling made "general tests" for houses, burials and miscellaneous features. Test areas consisted of a set of six parallel 1 m by 18 m trenches laid 3 m apart. These trenches were expanded as features were exposed. The location of these "general tests" is not made clear in the text, although they were mapped. There is no detailed discussion of excavation techniques used in the general testing, but it is clear that they were not as controlled as tests in Mounds 33 and 48 (Scantling 1940: 10). Scantling briefly noted that Mounds 2, 47, 51 and 52 were tested, but provided no detailed information on these mounds, noting only that the material recovered "compared favorably in every detail with that from the other two mounds tested and from the general testing" (Scantling 1940: 11).

Scantling uncovered the remains of 11 houses, about 40 outdoor hearths and three burials. His description (1940) of Jackrabbit Ruin material culture emphasized features (houses, floor features, outdoor hearths and roasting pits, and burials) and technological aspects of Sells Plain, Sells Red and Tanque Verde Red-on-brown pottery. Formal chipped and ground stone tools, shellwork and bone artifacts were more briefly described, but there is no information on chipped stone other than projectile points, drills, knives and "large blades" (fleshing knives). Scantling compared and contrasted material culture traits with those of the Gila Basin Hohokam, the Tucson Basin and the Salado cultures in order to define the origin and cultural affiliation of Jackrabbit Ruin. He concluded that similarities with the Salado were coincidence and that ties with Gila Basin Hohokam were weak, since only "non-basic" (Scantling 1940: 65) Hohokam traits were present at Jackrabbit Ruin. Scantling stressed the differences between Hohokam and Jackrabbit Ruin house types, pottery, stonework and burials and hypothesized that the Papaguería may be a northern extension of of unknown cultures to the south, rather than a southern extension of cultures to the north.

Under the auspices of the Arizona State Museum and the University of Arizona Department of Anthropology, field work also was undertaken at Valshni Village 14 miles southwest of Sells near the confluence of the Fresnal and Vamori (Valshni) washes. Scantling began limited testing in the spring of 1939. Arnold H. Withers and a Papago CCC-ID crew conducted more extensive excavations in the winter of 1939-1940. This project, which complements Scantling's investigations, resulted in the definition of the two Desert Hohokam phases preceding the Sells phase. Withers' (1941) master's thesis for the Department of Anthropology, University of Arizona, is devoted to discussion of the diagnostic traits of the Vamori and Topawa phases.

Valshni Village was evidenced on the surface by five trash mounds and "many" sherd concentrations covering an area of approximately 90,000 m^2. Using the methods devised for Jackrabbit Ruin, Withers excavated "stratitests" in four of the five mounds to obtain representative samples with which to construct a ceramic sequence for the site; the fifth mound was tested less systematically. Outside the mounds, an unspecified number of test areas were opened by digging

six parallel 1 m by 30 m trenches in the denser 30 m grid squares; Withers
does not mention whether dirt from these trenches was screened. Ceramics
were grouped by trench for analysis, suggesting that finer provenience
units were not used for excavation; however, Withers is not specific
on this point. The locations of the test areas are not provided. It is
not known, therefore, what proportion of the total site area was
excavated.

When features were encountered the trenches were expanded to
define the limits of the structure. The soil within the structures
was then removed to within 10 cm of the floor; the remaining soil was
removed as a single unit and the recovered artifacts were sacked
separately. Twenty-eight houses were excavated with these procedures.
Eighteen are attributed to the Vamori phase and seven to the Topawa
phase; presumably, no determination was made of the other three structures.

Several outdoor hearths, consisting of charcoal, rock and occasionally
of abundant animal bone also were excavated. Because the latter were
discussed as a group rather than individually, the exact number and configuration of these features and their relationships to the houses are
not known.

The format of Withers' thesis closely followed Scantling's
report; he described house types, hearths, outdoor roasting features and
a burial, and presented a technological analysis of the types of pottery
recovered through excavation. His analysis of "stonework" resembles
Scantling's, in that he focuses almost exclusively on easily recognized
formal ground and chipped stone tools, such as metates, manos, pestles,
axes, projectile points, scrapers, drills, knives and "blades" (fleshing
knives); other chipped stone items are not reported.

In his concluding chapter Withers lists the traits of the Vamori
and Topawa phases and concludes that these represent an earlier development
of the same culture which produced the Sells phase. He suggests that
the greater abundance of milling stone, the presence in the Baboquivari
valley of one and possibly two Sells phase irrigation canals, the increase in redware and the initial use of enclosures imply changes
during the Sells phase. Like Scantling, Withers hesitated to assign
a cultural affiliation to Valshni Village; he noted similarities in "non-
basic" items with the Gila Basin Hohokam, as well as ceramic affinities
with the Tucson Basin. He concluded that too little was known of areas
to the south and west to assess the relationship between them and Valshni
Village.

Scantling's and Withers' chief contribution is their description
of the three phases of what Haury (1950) later called the
Desert Hohokam. As noted previously, their reports are the baseline
for comparison with other excavations in the Papaguería, and are therefore, of continuing value to archaeologists. In this respect, the
archaeologists achieved their goals for developing a cultural-historical
framework. Despite this, the studies have deficiencies. There are

ambiguities and omissions in the discussion of excavation techniques in both reports. Scantling did not discuss all the tested areas or how they were selected for excavation. Excavations other than in Mound 33 are discussed in sketchy terms and information on the size of excavation units, the use of screens and the selection of artifacts for analysis is notably lacking. Although Withers' excavations appear to have been more systematic, the latter kinds of information also are lacking in his report. At the time of their investigations little attention was paid to non-diagnostic chipped stone items. As a result, lithic analyses today cannot use data from Jackrabbit Ruin and Valshni Village for comparative purposes.

While the reports are adequate for their time, new research interests and data recovery techniques make them deficient for today's research. A major focus of interest today is on relationships within areas of a site and between sites in a specified region. The former require finer provenience control and different sampling strategies than those employed by Scantling and Withers. In the two reports, culture traits are treated as measures of the degree of similarity between one region and another, but little effort was made to explain similarities and differences. A consideration of environmental conditions and trade and other political or economic relationships is lacking.

Differences between Jackrabbit Ruin and Valshni Village, such as the greater abundance of ground stone and the absence of mountain sheep at the former site, are attributed to change through time, but alternate explanations, such as different seasons of occupation, are not considered. Today's routine recovery techniques--the collection of pollen, flotation, radiocarbon and archaeomagnetic samples--did not exist when Jackrabbit Ruin and Valshni Village were dug. Finally, the very characteristics which made the two sites valuable for culture history questions--that is, their large size, density of artifacts and stratified deposits-- are somewhat anomalous for the Papaguería. It is highly likely, therefore, that these two settlements differed significantly from other smaller contemporaneous sites. Excavations in these smaller sites are critical to our understanding of the broader subsistence-settlement patterns and the relationship between the more common small sites and the more unusual larger villages.

In The Stratigraphy and Archaeology of Ventana Cave Haury (1950: 2-5) evaluated the results of a survey and the two excavations discussed above in order to point to deficiencies in the knowledge of Papaguerían prehistory. Based on the three phases defined through these excavations, Haury (1950: 6-13) defined the Desert branch of the Hohokam. Haury also drew from information on complexes described elsewhere, particularly from Rogers' work in southern California and Sayles and Antevs' work in southeastern Arizona, to interpret the archaeological remains at Ventana Cave. A description of the above culture phases and complexes, including Haury's Ventana Cave sequence, is to be found in Chapter 4.

Deficiencies in the excavation methods used at Ventana Cave
(Haury 1950: 47-50) are related to a refinement of archaeological
techniques since the time of its excavation in the early 1940s.
The use of 50 cm arbitrary levels when small natural stratigraphic
subdivisions were not evident would probably be considered excessive
today. However, Haury's (1950: 206) argument that the quantity and
duplication of materials helped to correct problems associated with the
mixture of levels by rodent and grave digging activities could probably
be extended to his use of deep arbitrary stratigraphic units as well.
Haury also points out that the procedure of analyzing most of the large
artifacts in the field and taking only a few "type" artifacts to the
lab may have resulted in the loss of some information. Because of
their large numbers, only the stone artifacts that fit within a system
of classification (for instance, "tools") were studied, leaving damaged
or unworked artifacts unanalyzed (Haury 1950: 171). Today the problem
of great volumes of artifacts would be dealt with by sampling all
classes of artifacts, including debitage. The use of pollen, flotation
and various absolute dating techniques were not available at that time,
although material from the lowest levels of Ventana Cave has since
been radiocarbon dated. These radiocarbon dates support the earlier
dating of the lowest cultural stratum based on geological and faunal
evidence (Haury 1975: preface). The excavation of Ventana Cave did
not fill in all of the gaps in our knowledge of the Papaguería, but it
did provide a framework upon which further research has been, and
will continue to be, designed.

The primary significance of this site hinges on the stratified
nature of its deposits. Stratified sites, a rare find in this desert
country, offer the most reliable means for reconstructing the past
culture history of an area. Anthropological approaches to archaeological
remains depend upon a knowledge of basic chronological and cultural
relationships. Research at Ventana Cave also is significant as a
pioneer effort at collaboration between the primary archaeologist, Haury,
and specialists in the analyses of geological deposits, soils, textiles,
human skeletal remains and faunal remains. In terms of the thoroughness
and balance with which the data are presented and evaluated, this report
set high standards for the study of Papaguería prehistory that
subsequent investigations have rarely met.

Research in the 1970s

In the 1970s research was resumed in the central Papaguería after
a hiatus of 25 years. The pace of research on the Papagueria increased
with the initiation of several contract projects by Arizona State
University (ASU), the Arizona State Museum and the National Park Service.
These investigations which are summarized and evaluated below, have
particular relevance to the Sells project area because of the focus on
small sites similar in configuration to those recently recorded near
Sells. Areas in and near the Santa Rosa and Tat Momoli valleys have
been the focus of three investigations: (1) Hecla's Lakeshore Mining

Project (ASU), (2) the Santa Rosa Wash Project (ASM), and (3) the Vekol Copper Mining Project (Prescott College and ASM). Summaries of these three investigations are excerpted from McClellan and Vogler (1977).

Investigations in the northeastern portion of the Papago Reservation were undertaken by ASM prior to construction of a Tucson Gas & Electric Company transmission line. Limited investigations on road rights-of-way throughout the Papagueria have been conducted by the National Park Service, the Arizona State Museum and Arizona State University. Wells and access roads near Kaka and Stoa Pitk also have been surveyed by the Arizona State Museum. These studies are summarized on the basis of published reports and unpublished site data and manuscripts on file at ASM and NPS. They have particular relevance to the Sells project area for the reasons cited above.

The Hecla Lakeshore Mining Project involved field operations in a 6 square mile area; field work began in December 1971 and was completed in fall of 1973. Goodyear's final report (1975) represents an attempt at a synchronic functional analysis in conjunction with a study of diachronic changes in the area. The study centered around subsistence-settlement patterning in the Slate Mountains, with the subject of human ecology being treated in detail.

The study area fell almost entirely within the palo-verde--saguaro community (see Lowe 1964: 24-6), which is noted for its high species diversity, particularly in relation to species of plants of high economic value. Goodyear developed a stratified archaeological sampling design for a large, continuous zone of study, which ran down the slopes of the Slate Mountains. Thus, the entire range of environmental settings within the area could be sampled without a bias toward one or the other of the environmental zones present. Linear plant transects were established to provide for the collection of quantifiable data relative to the types of vegetation communities present and their hypothesized carrying capacities.

Goodyear (1975: 236) notes that stratified archaeological sampling techniques based on present-day floral distributions are not advisable where environmental stress is suspected to have occurred, but the Slate Mountain area is thought to have been relatively unaffected by such stresses. As a result, he holds that his research approach can be justified. Goodyear (1975) concludes that on the basis of his study and others conducted in the Santa Rosa Wash, there appears to be an obvious relationship between the type and location of settlement patterns observed and the natural resources of the area.

In order to arrive at this conclusion, it was necessary that Goodyear assume a very close correlation between the past and the present environment of the Slate Mountains. While there is not enough paleoenvironmental data available at present to state categorically whether or not this assumption is valid, Goodyear cites considerable archaeological evidence from his study area that suggests that his assumption of relative environmental stability can be justified. Goodyear's work in the Slate Mountains is particularly important because it attempts to provide a better understanding of the archaeological materials in the area as records of past activities, especially as they relate to subsistence systems in a marginal environment.

The Santa Rosa Wash Project involved the survey of a 30 square mile parcel of land in the Santa Rosa Valley which was expected to be affected by construction of Tat Momolikot Dam, and the testing of three previously located archaeological sites in the proposed reservoir area. Field operations were begun in July 1972 under the supervision of Edward Germeshausen. The survey area was bounded on the north by the Tat Momoli Mountains, on the south by the Slate Mountains, and on the west by the Santa Rosa flood plain. The eastern boundary of the study area cut through the Tat Momoli Valley a short distance east of the Slate and Tat Momoli mountains (Canouts, Germeshausen and Larkin 1972).

Initial survey resulted in the location of 38 sites, with subsequent survey resulting in the location of 11 additional sites. The survey was intended to be intensive with the archaeological record of the area being viewed from an ecological perspective and employing the same interpretive model for both prehistoric and historic remains.

In evaluating the research potential of the cultural resources within the study area, Canouts, Germeshausen and Larkin defined five "problem domains"; these included (1) trails, (2) areas of lithic activity, (3) sherd and lithic scatters on the Santa Rosa flood plain, (4) the Tat Momolikot series of Papago village units, and (5) historic mining and related activities. These definitions of problem domains do not, strictly speaking, parallel the site-type categories frequently encountered in archaeological literature. Rather, they represent the relationship between the location of cultural materials and their probable behavioral correlate.

The first section of the report focuses on a determination of the cultural and environmental setting of the study area, with the remaining sections offering a definition and description of the problem domains in terms of the specific sites each includes. It is this section of the report that sets the stage for the in-depth analysis of the identified cultural resources presented by Raab (1974) in his preliminary report on Phase I of the Santa Rosa Wash Project.

Raab's report represents a research design aimed at mitigating the adverse effects of dam construction on the cultural resources of the upper Santa Rosa Wash. Raab generates and attempts to test a series of hypotheses designed to demonstrate that prehistoric settlement in the Santa Rosa Wash area was conditioned to a large degree by the distribution of prehistoric food resources. A total of 175 sites were investigated during Phase I, with data on settlement patterning being collected through survey, surface collection of cultural materials, and excavation.

An attempt to reconstruct probable prehistoric vegetation zones involved a large scale sampling program similar to that used by Goodyear on the Hecla Project. Inferences concerning prehistoric agriculture were made on the basis of data derived from soil tests and a regional evaluation of hydrological conditions. Much of the theoretical framework for Raab's Santa Rosa Wash study was based on his previous work with Goodyear on the Hecla Lakeshore Project.

The bulk of Raab's report is descriptive, providing a detailed account of the types of information collected and a statement of field method. A general statement of the results of the initial survey is included in the first portion of the report. The remaining sections of the report deal with an interpretation of the data collected and an evaluation of the theoretical and methodological bases for his research. Raab employs the concept of problem domains, as defined by Canouts, Germeshausen and Larkin, and views the cultural manifestations present in each problem domain in terms of their location relative to geologic formations and biotic communities.

On the basis of differential distribution of plant communities, Raab defined three environmental zones within the study area. These zones included the area surrounding Santa Rosa Wash, the Santa Rosa flood plain, and the lower slopes of the Slate Mountains. With this framework in mind, Raab defined a "core area" that encompassed the western slopes of the Slate Mountains, Santa Rosa Wash and its flood plain; thus the core area included every major physiographic and ecological zone in the project area. Subsequent analysis revealed that the core area was characterized by the highest site density of any portion of the study area.

In addition to differences in the type, size and distribution of sites relative to different environmental zones, Raab was able to demonstrate that flood plain sites contained lithic materials and macrobotanical remains that could only have come from geologic formations and biotic communities in the Slate Mountains (Raab 1974: 159).

Sites in the study area were dated by means of ceramic identification. The data derived from ceramics, when coupled with information available on site density and distribution, led Raab to the conclusion that the area had been occupied as early as A.D. 300, at which time sites first appeared on the Santa Rosa flood plain. The population of the area achieved its maximum density during the transition from the Santa Cruz phase (A.D. 700-900) to the Sacaton phase (A.D. 900-1100), during which time the largest and most numerous sites in the area were occupied. Raab hypothesizes a rapid population decline shortly after A.D. 900, although the area continued to be occupied until at least A.D. 1400 (Raab 1974: 301-02).

Raab concludes his report with the postulation of a three component settlement system for the Santa Rosa Wash study area. The three components, which are viewed as interdependent elements within a

larger generalized subsistence system, include (1) the flood plain
village component, characterized by base camps that served as the
nucleus of the system; (2) the mountain component, which witnessed
only seasonal use; and (3) the agricultural component. While Raab's
work cannot be considered conclusive, an impressive amount of archaeological and environmental data seems to support his conclusions.

As did Goodyear, it has been necessary for Raab to assume
that there has been no major shift either in the density or the distribution of biotic communities within his study area over the last 1000
years. As with Goodyear's study, archaeological data seem to indicate
that this assumption may be valid. The significance of Raab's work
rests not only in the fact that a great amount of specific and
quantified data was derived from his research, but also that his
research was carried out within a regional context. Raab had at his disposal not only the data retrieved from the Santa Rosa Wash study,
but also that collected by Goodyear in the Slate Mountains. It
might well have been impossible for Raab to offer his hypotheses
concerning settlement and subsistence in the Santa Rosa Wash area had he
chosen to use data from the study area only. By taking advantage of
the full range of information available for the surrounding areas,
Raab was able to offer a more comprehensive and better documented treatment
of the cultural resources of the Santa Rosa Wash area. At the same
time he minimized the need for introducing conjecture or untestable hypotheses into his analytic framework.

The final study to be examined in the area of Santa Rosa Wash
was prepared by Yvonne Stewart and Lynn Teague as part of the Vekol
Copper Mining Project (Stewart and Teague 1974). Their report
was prepared with the aim of assessing the impact of a proposed open
pit copper mine upon cultural resources within the proposed mining
area. The original Prescott College survey resulted in the location
of 63 archaeological sites within the 8 square mile area. A brief
reconnaissance of the study area later was carried out by the
Arizona State Museum, in order to establish the research base needed
for the assessment.

During the Prescott College field operations, prehistoric,
historic Papago and American Anglo cultural materials were identified.
Small sites that did not warrant excavation were completely collected.
Larger sites were "grab sampled," with all obvious artifacts collected
(Stewart and Teague 1974). The Prescott College data, coupled with
more specific data collected by the Arizona State Museum on several
sites and on the environmental context, allowed Stewart and Teague
to deal with the cultural resources of the area within the framework of human ecology.

In attempting to define the relationships existing between biotic,
abiotic, social and economic environments, Stewart and Teague proposed

(after Canouts, Germeshausen and Larkin 1972) six problem domains, or areas of potential research, for the archaeological resources of the area. In establishing their problem domains, sites were grouped into six categories based on available artifactual and environmental data. Problem Domain I included four types of gathering sites, defined on the basis of chronology, environmental setting, proximity to washes, site size and site density. Problem Domain II included base camps; Problem Domain III, trails; Problem Domain IV, whole vessels and trail breaks; Problem Domain V, the Reward Mine area; and Problem Domain VI, anomalous sites, or sites that did not fit into any of the previously defined categories.

Definitions of the various problem domains were accompanied by a set of postulates by which each might be tested during future field operations. The research strategy proposed by Stewart and Teague was intentionally left on a rather general level, so that the individual who chose to implement it might adapt it more readily to his specific research interests and expertise (Stewart and Teague 1974: 45). The remainder of the report deals with budget proposals, mitigation proposals and site descriptions.

A quick review of these studies reveals that each of them assumed an approach conducive to analysis in terms of human ecology. Cultural materials were viewed in terms of the dynamic processes involved in human behavior, rather than as static records of past events. These studies appear to be more productive than previous work in terms of understanding human behavior in the past. This is not to say that studies which focus on topics such as the reconstruction of culture sequences lack value, rather that analyses which consider the archaeological record in terms of the behavioral context in which it was produced tend to be more informative if one is hoping to understand an area's prehistory.

These studies in the Santa Rosa and Tat Momoli valleys exemplify a regional approach to prehistoric and historic activities and stand in contrast to the linear surveys discussed below, which can provide only fragmentary data on the environmental context of the sites and little documentation of the relationships between sites. While data from linear surveys can suggest possible functions of sites and relationships among the site and local resources and other sites, these can only be fully tested with regional data.

The remainder of this chapter is devoted to linear surveys and related data recovery operations conducted by ASM and WAC in the central Papaguería. These studies deal with the narrow transects of road and transmission line rights-of-way. Because of the inherent limitations of a linear survey or related data recovery, these undertakings usually focus on site-specific problems, such as site function, occupation dates and activity areas within sites. Broader problems, such as relationships among sites within a region, and the relationships between sites and the environment, usually receive lesser emphasis.

Additionally, investigations on linear projects sometimes may be limited by project conditions to small, arbitrarily selected portions of sites. This condition further restricts the confidence with which archaeologists can interpret the archaeological remains thus recovered.

The Arizona State Museum conducted studies prior to construction of the Tucson Gas and Electric Company (TG&E) El Sol to Vail transmission line. This 300-foot-wide corridor extends approximately 182 miles from an area west of Phoenix to just southeast of Tucson, crossing the Vekol, Santa Rosa and Avra valleys in the northeastern part of the Papago Reservation. In March and April of 1974 an ASM crew of four, headed by Ric Windmiller, surveyed the right-of-way and recorded 34 sites, of which 33 were given ASM site numbers. Three sites (AZ T:11:31, AZ AA:10:3, AZ AA:14:14) on which direct impact could not be avoided were recommended for further study; data recovery was later recommended for two additional sites, AZ AA:15:11 and AZ T:16:41.

While many microenvironments occur in the southern Arizona basin and range province, the transmission line right-of-way was confined to bajadas and outwash plains for most of its length and generally crossed, rather than paralleled rivers and washes. This resulted in an over-representation of bajada and outwash plains sites and an under-representation of sites occurring along washes and permanent streams, thereby limiting what could be learned about regional patterns of settlement and subsistence. In recognition of the inherent limitation of the survey, McDonald and others (1974) selected a broad cultural ecological research orientation rather than a specific research design. The authors focused on the relationship of the sites to specific environmental features (e.g. vegetation communities, lithic resources, water) based on the hypothesis that site locations are selected to minimize energy expended in acquiring resources while maximizing the potential for their acquisition. Next, the authors outlined four sets of activities--procurement, processing, distribution and consumption--and the array of artifacts and features characteristic of each set. These characteristics then were used to classify the recorded sites according to function.

McDonald and others (1974) attempted to examine patterns in site function and environment. In order to do so, they ranked riparian settings, palo-verde--saguaro, and creosote-bush--bur-sage communities in terms of their wild plant productivity and agricultural potential (carrying capacity). Based on previous knowledge of prehistoric subsistence patterns, the authors ranked riparian settings highest in plant productivity, followed by palo-verde--saguaro communities. Creosote-bush--bur-sage communities were less productive, but portions were more suitable than the other zones for ak chin, or irrigation, farming. Correlating site function with environmental data, the authors found that all 12 primary habitation villages, or rancherías were located in river terraces on alluvial plains adjacent to washes (McDonald and others 1974: 46), where wild plant productivity and agricultural

potential are highest. The authors also found patterning of sites
that show evidence of quarrying or plant procurement and quarrying.
Five such sites cluster in the western foothills of the Sierra
Estrella, where quartzite nodules are available; the remaining two
are found in the Silverbell and Roskruge mountains not far from
desert Hohokam habitation areas and near rhyolite outcrops.

The authors also attempted to differentiate between wild and
domestic plant harvesting and processing sites. These patterns are
less convincing than the patterns in habitation and quarry sites.
For example, processing sites were differentiated from procurement
loci by the presence of ground stone. This rested on the assumption
that collected plants were brought to processing areas at which
grinding implements were available because it is inefficient to
carry heavy ground stone to collecting areas. In reality, the archaeological differences between prehistoric collecting and processing
loci are probably more blurred, particularly in view of the possibility
that reusable items, including metates, were removed when collecting
and processing camps were abandoned (Stacy 1974: 78). McDonald and
others (1974) also differentiate between domestic and wild plant
procurement and processing; however, this distinction is based on the
somewhat circular argument that because creosote-bush--bur-sage communities
are more suitable for ak chin farming and saguaro--palo-verde communities
have a higher wild plant productivity, similar assemblages within the
two communities reflect domestic and wild plant use, respectively.

Aside from the minor flaws in assumptions and logic noted above,
a final question regarding the identification of site function from
survey data is raised by the survey methods employed on the El Sol to
Vail project. At that time the survey forms in use by ASM required
a narrative summary of features and artifact assemblages, but did not
specifically call for quantitative observations; it is therefore
questionable whether the surveyors made the thorough, consistent
observations needed for an accurate assessment of site function. In
light of the fact that 182 miles were surveyed in six weeks, the corre-
lations between site function and environment should be viewed as
highly tentative.

Although their reconstruction of prehistoric activities must
be regarded as hypothetical at this point, the authors of the El Sol
to Vail report are to be commended for their effort to transcend the
limitations of linear surveys; the regional perspective provided in this
report contrasts favorably with the narrow focus seen in many linear
survey reports.

Data recovery for the Tucson Gas & Electric El Sol to Vail
project took place in August 1974 and between January and March 1976.
Because of planning constraints, these studies were undertaken by
four different supervisors. As a result, the investigations are
somewhat lacking in overall continuity and consistency in research
approach, field methods and analysis. To date, only the 1974 data

recovery operations are published; the remaining studies will be published in 1979. The published and unpublished reports are discussed below.

In August 1974 Joel Johnstone and Martin Rose (ASM) made limited collections and test excavations at two lithic sites, ASM AZ T:11:31 and ASM AZ AA:10:3. At each site a 5 m by 5 m grid system was laid over a portion of the scatter and 10 randomly selected squares were collected and tested. Since no evidence of cultural deposits or features was found, operations were terminated. These efforts yielded 33 pieces of chipped stone from 0.5 percent of the surface area of AZ T:11:31 and 154 pieces from 2.5 percent of the surface area of AZ AA:10:3.

These data recovery efforts were reported by Spain (1975) who analyzed the lithic collections from the two sites. Using a behavioral chain model developed by Phillips in McDonald and others (1974), Spain succinctly outlined two sets of test implications, one for lithic procurement and manufacture and the other for lithic use, maintenance and discard; he then attempted to test the hypothesis that the two lithic scatters represented procurement and manufacturing loci quarries. While Spain's model is sound, his lithic analysis is not; the sample size is far too small, the lithic typology is vaguely defined, the techniques of analysis are not discussed, and the presentation of quantitative data is confusing. Together, these deficiencies preclude any evaluation of the conclusion that these sites are quarries.

Data recovery from another lithic site, AZ AA:15:11, was more productive. Linford (n.d.) defined his site as an elliptical 105 m by 80 m area in and near the transmission line corridor, but noted that smaller and/or less dense clusters extended at least one-half mile in a northwesterly direction. It is possible therefore, that Linford actually was dealing with an arbitrarily defined portion of a much larger site area. Using a 5 m by 5 m grid system, Linford and his crew collected 75 of the possible 320 squares within the defined collection area. Although this represents 23.4 percent of the collection area, a somewhat larger fraction of the total number of artifacts probably was collected, since grids within visible concentrations were deliberately selected for collection. The crew also excavated and screened deposits from a 10 cm deep 1 m by 2 m test pit and a 20 cm deep 1 m by 1 m pit; since extremely few artifacts were recovered, further test excavations were not undertaken. In his analysis of the 1127 lithics recovered from the site, Linford attempted to determine overall site function and to define spatially and temporally distinct concentrations within the site. Using Spain's report as a point of departure, Linford developed test implications for site function, as well as for the presence or absence of functionally or temporally discrete areas within the site. Based on these test implications, he outlined a lithic typology and a series of attributes he planned to use for the study. The numbers and percentages of items in each artifact category are shown in various tables in the report. Linford reviewed the data in light of the test implications and concluded that the data strongly supported the hypothesis that the site was an area of lithic procurement and preliminary manufacture.

Linford's analysis of overall site function is, on the whole, satisfactory, his logical arguments relating to site function are sound, and the variables selected for a functional study are appropriate. His attention to the recovery of visible clusters as analytical units is commendable. The one questionable aspect of his functional analysis is his treatment of utilized flakes; these materials were assigned functions according to the kinds of motions (scraping, cutting, reaming, gouging) assumed to be responsible for producing observed microwear patterns. Since exact correspondences between the use of an artifact and microwear patterns remain to be established, the validity of Linford's approach is questionable. The difficulties in interpreting microwear are compounded by the fact that the surface materials were collected from some areas disturbed by jeep trails. Additionally, the granular rhyolites and basalts that comprise the lithic assemblage are materials on which microwear is difficult to identify, a fact to which the high percentage (21 percent) of "possibly utilized flakes" attests.

Linford's second goal was to determine whether the visible artifact concentrations represented distinct activities or events. Artifacts from four of the six concentrations exceeding a density of 15 items per 25 m^2 were selected for comparison; distributions of raw materials and classes of artifacts are presented in various tables. Linford then evaluated the data in terms of the proposed test implications and concluded that the concentrations were independent chipping events. While it is logical to interpret the scatter as a frequently revisited limited use area, the proof for this is elusive. The strongest evidence for this interpretation is the differential distribution of such raw materials as quartzite and meta-sediment; however the fact that miscellaneous rhyolites are the dominant raw materials in all four clusters suggests that the clusters are rather similar. Linford noted significant differences between clusters in the distribution of soft and hard hammer flakes, retouch flakes, pebble tools, cores, and hammerstones and retouched artifacts (Linford n.d.: Table 5), indicating that chipping activities varied among loci. The distribution of utilized specimens is less convincing, particularly in view of the fact that the tool categories in question are comprised largely of utilized flakes, to which it is extremely difficult to assign functions (compare Linford n.d.: Tables 1 and 5). Linford suggests that differences in the sizes and densities of the concentrations may indicate functional or temporal differences in chipping activity. Although there are minor differences in density (which ranges from 1.11 to 2.1 artifacts per square meter) and in concentration size (which ranges from 75 to 150 m^2), it is questionable whether these differences are meaningful.

In summary, Linford's argument that the site represents lithic procurement and manufacturing, rather than lithic use, maintenance and discard, is supported by the data. He was not able to demonstrate that the clusters represent separate chipping activities, although differential distribution of raw materials and soft and hard hammer flakes are suggestive. Linford's combination of utilized flakes with formal tool types (Linford n.d.: Table 1) is questionable, but it does not invalidate the conclusion that the site represents lithic procurement and tool manufacturing.

In January and February 1976, Shenk and Coston (n.d.) conducted mitigation studies at AZ AA:14:14, a sherd and lithic scatter in the Viopuli drainage some 30 miles northeast of Sells; their research focused on general questions of culture history and site function. The archaeologists established a 30 m by 30 m grid system over the site thus creating about 60 whole squares and 29 partial squares. Recognizable surface concentrations were collected as features within the grids; remaining materials were grouped by grid provenience. A total of 37 contiguous grids (placed over the central portion of the site) were collected and eight features were identified.

Features 1 through 4 and 8 were scatters of varying density; at least two of these concentrations were tested for subsurface cultural material. Three test pits were placed in Feature 2, which contained a concentration of fire-cracked rock, but little evidence of subsurface material was found. Two pits were placed in Feature 8, a scatter eroding out of an arroyo; this, too, showed no evidence of cultural material below a depth of 20 cm.

More detailed studies focused on a 30 m by 60 m area containing three trash concentrations (Features 5, 6, and 7) which was the major zone of occupation within the site. Each 30 m square was subdivided into 2 m squares, of which a 10 percent sample was systematically selected for excavation. In all, 46 of the possible 450 squares were excavated in 10 cm arbitrary levels; deposits were passed through a one-quarter-inch mesh screen, and pollen and flotation samples were collected.

Testing beneath Feature 7 revealed a 90 cm deep trash pit without vertical stratigraphy. Two, possibly three, hearths and two probable post holes were discovered beneath Feature 5; these associated features were interpreted as the remains of one, or possibly two, separate occupation or household structures built on the surface.

The detailed descriptive analysis of the 9,256 sherds, 1,527 lithics, 67 bone fragments and 4 pieces of shell was designed to facilitate comparisons with assemblages from Ventana Cave, Jackrabbit Ruin and Valshni Village. Ceramics were classified by previously defined types; when possible, vessel shapes were identified. Lithics were classified on the basis of a series of formal attributes; flake size, edge angles and lengths of utilized edges of tools were measured. From this activities reflective of habitation were identified. An analysis of the horizontal distribution of the lithics showed no correlation between specific activities and specific artifact concentrations. Shenk and Coston briefly discuss the faunal and shell remains. Most faunal material was too poorly preserved for a species identification; the few identifiable fragments were from rabbits and deer. In terms of kinds of animal bone, AZ AA:14:14 was found to resemble Jackrabbit Ruin. Shell consisted of 2 Glycymeris bracelet fragments, a ring made of a thin band of Conus shell and a fragment of Glycymeris manufacturing debris.

Shenk and Coston evaluate and summarize their findings in light of what is currently known about Papaguerían prehistory. Based on the presence of Sells Plain, Tanque Verde Red-on-brown with early design elements, and a low percentage of Sells Red, the site was dated to the early Sells phase, about A.D. 1200-1300. The authors concluded that the site is a single occupation agricultural site. Regrettably, the pollen and flotation analyses that might confirm this interpretation have not been undertaken.

On balance, Shenk and Coston provide a straightforward, thorough analysis of material culture. Their primary contribution to questions of Papaguería culture history and settlement and subsistence is the provision of a baseline against which other small sites can be compared. In contrast to many corridor studies, Shenk and Coston were able to investigate almost the entire site and could, therefore, view features within the site as functional parts of the entire occupation; as a result, their interpretations of site function and the site's position in a regional subsistence system is more reliable than inferences made from more limited excavations.

AZ T:16:41, a site consisting of two areas of sherd and lithic scatter on the bajada west of the Sierra Estrella Mountains, was the final TG&E El Sol to Vail site to be investigated by the Arizona State Museum. An unpublished report by the supervisor (Curriden n.d.a) briefly discusses field methods and the results of the ceramic and lithic analyses.

First, 20 m by 20 m grids were laid out over the scatter; all grids were collected after 4 discernible clusters (Curriden n.d.a: Figure 3) were recorded and mapped. Feature 2, a rock-lined hearth, and Feature 3, a circular alignment of stones believed to be a pot or basket support, were visible on the surface. Trench 12 and an unnumbered unit were excavated to define these features. Ten additional meter squares within the larger scatter and two within the smaller scatter were dug to a depth of 10 cm. With the exception of Trenches 4 and 5, in which Feature 1, a rock-lined hearth similar to Feagure 2 was found, these grids were sterile immediately below the present ground surface of desert pavement. Curriden's (n.d.a: IV-11) only comment on sampling is that these grids "were chosen in a stratified random manner (one per 20 m^2 where warranted)," is ambiguous, and it remains unclear exactly how areas were selected for excavation.

Curriden initially proposed several hypotheses for testing; these focused on the function of the site, the relationship of the scatter to local biotic resources, intrasite variability, and the relationship of the site to nearby possible trails. The latter two were later excluded from consideration because of the extensive sheet wash disturbance and the lack of diagnostic artifacts in association with the trails.

Curriden reported that 728 sherds and 5 lithics were recovered. She noted that the painted ceramics date between A.D. 590 and 1100 and that at least one plainware sherd dates from the Classic period (Curriden n.d.a: IV-25). She also concluded that the small scatter represented at least four painted vessels (of which three were flare-rimmed bowls) and four plainware vessels; the larger scatter contained at least one plainware jar. From this evidence, it is apparent that Curriden performed a fairly traditional ceramic analysis and classified sherds by existing ceramic types and vessel forms. Since five flakes were the only lithics recovered from the site, Curriden simply described these artifacts, an approach that is certainly adequate for such a small, undiagnostic sample. Curriden concluded that the site was a temporary collecting area, an interpretation which seems in line with the findings she reported.

Curriden's research goals and field methods appear to be adequate, given the limited materials on the site. The brevity of her report and the fact that it remains unpublished limit its value to other researchers.

As a group, the TG&E data recovery operations have so far added little to the prehistory of the Papaguería, either because the investigations are wholly inadequate (Spain 1975) or because the data remain unpublished. Shenk and Coston's manuscript has wider applicability than the other reports, first because the analysis was designed for comparison with other sites, and second, because of the abundance of small Sells phase scatters throughout the Papaguería similar to Shenk and Coston's site. Linford's manuscript, though not without problems, is of value because comparatively little work has been done with lithic scatters on the Reservation. Although Curriden's report is an adequate treatment of a limited activity site, it is, because of its brevity, less useful than the others for general purposes.

In addition to the previously mentioned area near Sells, the National Park Service and institutions under contract to it conducted survey and data recovery throughout the Reservation for the Papago Indian Roads Project between 1973 and 1977. These efforts and the related reports are listed in Table 5. Because of the current emphasis on recording small ephemeral sites, as well as the larger scatters, this

Table 5. Papago Indian Roads Survey and Data Recovery: 1973-1977.

Project	Agency or Institution	Reference
Papago Indian Roads Survey		
San Vicente to Queen's Well	NPS	Stacy (1973, 1975)
Highway 15 to Ventana Junction	NPS	Stacy (1973)
Highway 86 to Pisinimo	NPS	Stacy (1973)
Highway 86 to Hickiwan	NPS	Stacy (1973)
Sells to Gu Oidak (Big Fields); PIR 24	NPS	Stacy (1973, 1975)
Hickiwan to Kaka	NPS	Not reported
Route 86 to Ali Chuk	NPS	Jones (1974)
Ali Chukson access	NPS	Somers (1975)
San Miguel	NPS	Somers (1975)
Topawa Streets	NPS	Somers (1975)
Noliak to Haivan Nakya Loop	NPS	Somers (1975)
Charco 27	NPS	Somers (1975)
State Highway 86-Pan Tak	NPS	Somers (1975)
Santa Rosa Ranch School to Sil Nakya	NPS	Done 1973; no report
State Highway 86 to Viopuli	NPS	Somers (1975)
Pisinimo to Kom Vo	NPS	Somers (1975)
Gu Oidak to Cowlic	NPS	Somers (1975)
Route 19 to Vamori	NPS	Done 1973: no report
Vaiva Vo to Kohatk	ASU	P. Brown (1976)
Kom Vo to Papago Farms	ASM	Ferg and Vogler (1977)
Papago Indian Roads Data Recovery		
Santa Rosa to Ventana	NPS	Masse (in prep.)
Noliak to Haivan Nakya Loop	NPS	Rosenthal (n.d.)
Pisinimo to San Simon	NPS	No report
Charco 27	ASM	Vogler (1978)
Kom Vo to Papago Farms	ASM	Vogler (1978)
State Road 86 to Ali Chuk	NPS	Rosenthal and others (1978)
Vaiva Vo to Kohatk	ASU	Yablon (1978)

project had the potential for providing updated comparative data from most of the major basins on the Reservation. Due to limitations inherent in the right-of-way studies and to the incomplete publication of data obtained from these efforts, the potential of this project has not been fully realized.

Survey efforts have been summarized by Stacy (1973), Jones (1974), Somers (1975), Stacy (1975), P. Brown (1976) and Ferg and Vogler 1977); the first three, all unpublished manuscripts on file at Western Archeological Center, consist of very brief site descriptions and management recommendations. Together, the unpublished and published reports provide important documentation of the long-term (Archaic to modern) use of the Papaguería and many include data on historic Papago and Anglo sites. The inclusion of historic Papago and Anglo resources represents a significant departure from previous survey efforts, which were devoted primarily to prehistoric phenomena.

In 1973 Pheriba Stacy and three trainees surveyed five rights-of-way in four basins on the Papago Reservation. According to Stacy, these routes, summarized in Table 5, were confined to the flood plains drained by the following washes: the Aguirre, Santa Rosa, San Simon, Hickiwan (a tributary of the San Simon Wash), and Sells. As the rights-of-way did not cross bajadas and mountain zones, no new information on cultural resources in these settings was obtained. Information on survey methods, cultural resources and environmental settings are found in Stacy (1973). A summary article with wider distribution (Stacy 1975) presents general survey findings, integrated with previous knowledge of prehistory on the Papaguería. The survey resulted in the discovery of two sites, consisting of stone circles without surface artifacts, and 23 surface sherd and lithic scatters. Seven of the latter were tested for additional information of stratigraphy and subsurface features. Stacy did not discuss the sites individually, but outlined trends in the survey data. These were:

1) none of the scatters predates the Santa Cruz phase of the Hohokam sequence;
2) all scatters are single component surface sites without vertical stratigraphy;
3) with the exception of a single site on Santa Rosa Wash containing Santa Cruz and Sacaton painted ceramics, those sites with decorated wares all contained red-on-brown painted pottery;
4) all scatters contained non-micaceous plainwares, but were devoid of redwares;
5) surface features, if present, consisted of concentrations of artifacts or fire-cracked rock;
6) subsurface features consisted of hearths or roasting pits, sometimes associated with stained living areas and sherd concentrations; no structures were found;
7) features within a site were often separated by hundreds or thousands of feet and appeared in blade cuts (rather than in tested areas), an indication that test pits were not effective for discovering these dispersed features;
8) all but one site were less than one-half mile in diameter.

On the basis of the above trends, Stacy interpreted these ceramic sites as dispersed, late prehistoric settlements. Stacy also noted that sites were equally divided between locations near a hill or series of hills and locations away from hills on the alluvial valley floor. This pattern apparently does not reflect site function alone, since the pattern held even when large villages, small sherd and lithic scatters and camp sites were analyzed separately (Stacy 1975: 185). Stacy found that the valley floor sites either were between two large washes and within one-half mile of one of them, or within one-half mile of a single major wash in an area where the stream bed formed a dendritic pattern (Stacy 1975: 185). These locations resemble the 19th century Papago village locations, leading Stacy to suggest that a pattern similar to the 19th century semiannual settlement in field and well villages also existed during the late prehistoric period. The patterns in site location relative to washes and hills are especially important for planning purposes, since they may help predict archaeologically sensitive areas.

Stacy's study represents an update of Desert Hohokam trends outlined by Haury (Haury 1950). Although the right-of-way survey is a biased sample, in that it was confined to a single physiographic zone, it does not have the biases of pre-World War II surveys against recording small sherd and lithic scatters and isolated features; therefore, it adds to the understanding of the range of variability in sites in the Papaguería. Most importantly, Stacy observed that most ceramic period sites on the Papaguería lack vertical stratigraphy and diagnostic decorated ceramics, the two traditional tools for understanding prehistoric chronology, and called for the use of alternate techniques--archaeomagnetic, pollen, and dendrochronological studies, and the use of temper and vessel shape changes instead of surface design--for chronological control on sites on the Papaguería. These findings, combined with her observation that limited testing was not effective for discovering features, point out the need for modifying current field approaches to prehistoric sites on the Papago Reservation.

In January 1977 Ferg and Vogler (1977) surveyed an 11.75 mile route (PIR 21) from Kom Vo to Papago Farms in Kom Vo Valley, a southern extension of the Quijotoa Valley. They identified seven sites and 35 isolated artifacts. In addition to a background summary on the environment, previous research and relevant prehistory, their report provides a discussion of survey methods and recording procedures, descriptions and evaluations of the seven sites, and recommendations for data recovery at Sonora C:3:2. The authors report that all seven sites had prehistoric ceramic components; one of these also had an Archaic component, another contained materials from the 1920s, and a third contained both Archaic and early (pre-1860s?) Papago items. With the exception of Sonora C:3:2, a dense prehistoric sherd and lithic scatter, the sites were small, low density scatters. The findings from this survey confirm previous interpretations by Stacy (1975) and Haury (1950) that Papaguería sites usually are small, late prehistoric surface manifestations.

Data recovery related to the Papago Indian Roads Project has consisted largely of poorly documented surface collections and limited test excavations. Stacy tested six sites and found little evidence of stratified deposits; these excavations are not described fully in her summary article. Testing was undertaken at a site near Pisinimo by National Park Service personnel, but none of the remains have been reported or analyzed. Information on other PIR studies will be available in the future.

John Clonts collected and tested the road right-of-way portion of Gu Achi, a large village in the Santa Rosa drainage with relatively abundant Gila Basin buffware ceramics dating between A.D. 500 and 1100. Masse mapped the remainder of the site, collected a small sample of diagnostic materials outside the right-of-way, and is now preparing a report of this study. Data recovery of sites between Vaiva Vo and Kohatk is the subject of a master's thesis in preparation by Ronald Yablon, a graduate student at Arizona State University. This thesis is not available at this time.

Rosenthal (n.d.) briefly reported data recovery from AZ AA:13:21, a site discovered by Somers (1975) near the modern village of Comobabi, 11 miles northeast of Sells. The archaeologists collected the portion of the site in and just adjacent to the right-of-way, using 5 m by 5 m collection grids. The site, which was located in a zone with mesquite, saguaro, prickly-pear, cholla and jojoba, contained three concentrations within the right-of-way and historic features outside the right-of-way. It resembled food collecting and processing sites described by Goodyear (1975).

Rosenthal reported that 32 plainware sherds, 32 cores, 3 hammer-stones, 135 flakes, 2 preceramic period projectile points and 8 ground stone fragments were recovered from the sites. An unspecified number of early 20th century materials also were obtained. Rosenthal's descriptive analysis focused on questions of culture history and site function. Based on the assemblage and on the site location, Rosenthal concluded that the site represented a winter collecting, rather than a summer farming, locus.

As with remains from most sites investigated for the Papago Indian Roads Project, the remains collected from this site represent an arbitrary sample; it is impossible to assess whether the sample is representative of the rest of the site, since information on the portions outside the right-of-way is lacking. As far as the collected sample is concerned, Rosenthal's methods, analytical approach and inferences seem sound.

Reports by Vogler (1978) and Rosenthal and others (1978) are the only two published accounts of data recovery on the Papago Indian Roads Project. Both reports deal with sites in the Quijotoa Valley. Vogler (ASM) summarized data recovery operations undertaken in November 1977 at Sonora C:3:2 and AZ Z:14:47 under the supervision of Lynette Shenk. These studies were made in order to determine the research potential of these sites prior to road construction. Shenk's and Vogler's goals were to determine the function and temporal/cultural affiliation of the two sites, to ascertain the presence of sub-surface materials and to evaluate the eligibility of these sites for nomination to the National Register of Historic Places. In order to meet these goals, Shenk and Vogler were allowed to investigate the entire site area, rather than the right-of-way portion alone. They were, therefore, able to select collection and excavation areas on the basis of archaeological considerations, rather than solely on the basis of the impact of road construction.

Similar field procedures were used at both sites: site boundaries were defined, all visible surface features were mapped, and 5 m^2 collection grids were established in denser portions of the site. After surface collections were obtained, most surface features were excavated and areas of possible deposition were tested. All test pits were excavated in 10 cm levels unless natural stratigraphic units were dis-cernible; all excavated dirt was screened. Excavations within features were carried into sterile soil; elsewhere, test pits were terminated at a depth of 10 cm unless materials were of a sufficient quantity to warrant further excavation.

At Sonora C:3:2, 40 percent of the site area, or approximately 75 to 80 percent of the artifact inventory, was collected. Testing in the three possible features indicated (1) that the artifact con-centration was a surface deposit, (2) that a mounded area was a natural phenomenon, and (3) that a circular arrangement of partially buried stones was a hearth. Pollen and flotation samples of the latter are stored at the Arizona State Museum for future analysis.

AZ Z:14:47 (Hotasson Vo 4) was first thought by Somers (1975) to be a buried Classic period village near Sikort Chuapo Wash in the Quijotoa Valley. In order to test this interpretation, 66 5 m^2 grids were laid out in the denser portion of the site, which represented approximately one-seventh of the total site area (Vogler 1978: Figure 2). Eight features were defined within the surface scatter: an artifact con-centration; a mano and associated metate; 3 hearths; a possible hearth; a rectangular or oval structure partially defined by an alignment of stones, and a stone circle. All but the associated mano and metate and the possible hearth were tested, and two additional pits were excavated outside the features. These excavations revealed that the site was a surface scatter rather than a buried village, and suggested that the structure and stone circle were the remains of windbreaks or temporary shelters.

Vogler's artifact analyses were preliminary studies designed to indicate the range of activities performed at the site. Ceramics were classified according to established pottery types, and the range of vessel shapes represented in the collections was noted. Lithics were classified by raw material types and by broad formal categories (flakes, cores, formal tools). Tables show ceramic and lithic counts by type and provenience. Provenience data also are given for the few shell and bone fragments recovered from the two sites.

Based on field interpretations and on artifact analyses, Vogler interprets both sites as short term Sells phase specialized activity sites. Sonora C:3:2 centered around the seasonal procurement of plant resources, perhaps with occasional on-site processing; the primary focus of AZ Z:14:47 was the processing of vegetal resources (possibly mesquite pods).

Vogler provides a useful baseline for the comparison of small late Classic period sites on the Papaguería. The attention to features within the site and to the site as a whole yield a reliable picture of site activities. In this regard, it is important to note that Vogler was able to provide evidence for different kinds of activities at the two sites, even with unsophisticated preliminary artifact studies. Vogler's report of data recovery techniques and analyses is thorough and his conclusions are well argued. His report adds useful information on the configuration, stratigraphy and material remains which may be expected on Sells phase sites.

Rosenthal and others (1978) report data recovery and analysis at 11 sites on PIR 1 between State Highway 86 and Ali Chuk, and one site east of Hickiwan on PIR 34. All of these sites are in portions of the Quijotoa Valley (San Simon drainage). The PIR 1 sites represent approximately one-quarter of the 41 loci discovered on the PIR 1 right-of-way; the sites subject to data recovery were those resources that could not be avoided and that warranted further study.

This report on data recovery is divided into seven chapters: environmental and prehistoric background; research objectives; field methods; site descriptions; artifact analysis; discussion, and conclusions. These are followed by appendices concerned with analyses of faunal remains, pollen and other soil samples, human skeletal remains, and radiocarbon and archaeomagnetic samples. Discussions of specialized ceramic analyses and statistical methods also are included.

Using a research framework adapted from Stewart and Teague (1974), Rosenthal and others (1978) addressed basic questions of changing arid land adaptations over time and questions of Quijotoa Valley culture history. Their specific aims were to determine (1) the presence and nature of Paleo-Indian, Archaic and Ceramic occupations in the Quijotoa Valley; (2) the nature of Riverine Hohokam influence in the Quijotoa Valley; (3) the validity of Ezell's (1955) concept of the Sonoran Brownware tradition; (4) the presence or absence of continuity in tool traditions between the Archaic and Ceramic periods; and (5) the presence or absence of transition from the prehistoric to historic cultural traditions (Rosenthal and others 1978: 22-3). In addition, the researchers hoped to document activities performed at the sites, based on the assumption that site location reflected the use of local resources and that the character and configurations of the artifact assemblages reflected site functions.

In Chapter III Douglas Brown outlined field methods employed on the project. With the exception of AZ Z:11:5, which was divided into 5-foot squares, the right-of-way portions of the scatters were divided into 5 m^2 grids for surface collections and into 2 m^2 grids for test pit excavations. All features within the right-of-way were sampled and excavated using 10 cm arbitrary levels in the absence of discernible stratigraphy. All excavated soil was passed through a one-quarter-inch mesh screen and pollen and flotation samples were collected from appropriate proveniences. Although these field procedures are adequate, the reliability of the findings is somewhat reduced because the investigators were required by the Bureau of Indian Affairs to confine survey, collections and excavation to the 100 foot-wide road right-of-way.

In Chapter IV Brown provided a site-by-site description of the local setting, surface features, field procedures, and interpretations of site function based on field impressions. While this section suffices as a discussion of survey findings, it is not an adequate account of data recovery since findings from the artifact analyses were not incorporated in site interpretations.

Chapter V contains analyses of ceramics (Severson), chipped stone, ground stone, shell (Rosenthal) and bone artifacts (White). Severson's basic approach to the ceramics appears sound: he first separated plainwares from the more diagnostic materials (rim sherds, redwares, decorated wares, worked sherds and miscellaneous items) for analysis. He then classified plainwares into general types (Sells Plain, Gila Plain, Wingfield Plain, Lower Colorado buffware) and coded various attributes of surface treatment, temper and decoration. The deficiencies in his analysis are in data presentation and interpretations. In his data presentation, there are discrepancies between Table 7 (sherd tabulations) and the body of the discussion (Rosenthal and others 1978: 121-26). One site, Sonora C:2:15, appears in the site discussion, but is omitted from Table 7; two other sites, AZ Z:14:22 and AZ Z:14:40, appear in the discussion, but are not mentioned elsewhere in the report; four sites, Sonora C:2:25, AZ Z:14:25, AZ Z:14:23, and AZ Z:14:31, are listed in Table 7 but are not discussed in Severson's interpretations. The latter two are not described by Brown in Chapter IV. Severson's discussion of the individual sites (Rosenthal and others 1978: 121-26) does not take into account information provided by Brown in Chapter IV. As a result, multi-component sites, such as AZ Z:14:33, are misleadingly interpreted as single phase sites. The discussion of the data (Chapter VI) compounds errors in the text; Sonora C:2:15 and C:2:25, the two sites to which Yuma III or Yuma III and Papago remains are attributed (Rosenthal and others 1978: 213), do not have Colorado buffware ceramics of any period according to Severson's ceramic analysis. These discrepancies in the data and the failure to weigh ceramic data with other information available on these sites seriously undermine the reliability of Severson's site interpretations.

Severson does not succeed in his aim (Rosenthal and others 1978: 87) to support Ezell's formulation of the Sonoran brownware tradition; rather, he simply accepted his terminology without question and offered little independent evidence favoring this formulation. Severson (Rosenthal and others 1978: 128) seems to have chosen to emphasize, as Ezell did, the technological differences between Sonoran brownwares and Gila Basin buffwares rather than similarities in vessel shape and design.

Rosenthal investigated stages of lithic manufacture and patterns of wear in order to elicit information on artifact function and site activities. Her lithic typology is, for the most part, well defined and is suited to her interest in stages of core reduction and flake production, although a few categories (such as "retouched cores") are ambiguous. However, her data are extremely difficult to use for comparative purposes because more traditional formal chipped stone tool categories (other than projectile points) were not incorporated in the analysis. Aside from discrepancies and errors (Rosenthal and others 1978: 150 and Table 11; Figures 46, 47), the chief difficulty in this analysis is its format. Because the discussion is divided into sections by artifact category, it is almost impossible to extract data on individual sites. As a result of the author's focus on characteristics of the Quijotoa Valley collections as a whole rather than on the individual sites, the reader cannot obtain a clear picture of the variations among the sites in terms of assemblages, artifact density, features, site size or cultural-temporal affiliation. Tables summarizing these basic data by site would have remedied the problem and increased the usefulness of the report to other workers.

While the shell and bone analyses are organized in the same way, they present fewer problems simply because they deal with a much smaller body of data.

Chapter VI (Discussion) and VII (Conclusions), which comprise only 12 of the more than 300 pages of this report, are far too brief to adequately integrate the data presented in previous chapters. Although the authors present a summary of their findings, their general conclusions are so poorly linked to earlier chapters that one cannot evaluate their validity.

In addition to problems in organization, the report is flawed by erroneous or puzzling interpretations. Some of these are misinterpretations of existing knowledge. The authors misinterpret Haury's statement (Haury 1950: 319-20) regarding an absence of change in Cochise culture grinding stones in the Papaguería as an absence of typical Cochise culture grinding stones (Rosenthal and others 1978: 18). Redware ceramics do not first appear in the Topawa phase, as Rosenthal and others assert (1978: 19), but in the previous Vamori phase (Haury 1950: 6-19). Valshni Village does not, as Rosenthal and others (1978: 19) would have it, contain materials from all three phases, but only from the Vamori and Topawa phases (Withers 1941: 2).

Rosenthal and others (1978: 214) seem to imply, incorrectly, that the Desert Hohokam and Sonoran Brownware are two different traditions when they are, in fact, two different levels of interpretation of the same material culture evidence. Ezell's Sonoran Brownware formulation is a grouping of certain kinds of technologically similar ceramics found on the Papaguería in the prehistoric and historic periods; this formulation emphasizes the continuity in brownwares over time and their distinctiveness from buffwares. Haury's formulation of the Desert Hohokam (Haury 1950: 546-48) is an attempt to explain similarities and differences in ceramics and other items of material culture in the Papaguería and the Gila Basin. Haury suggests that these differences derive from different adaptations required by the two settings. Rosenthal's argument for using the Sonoran Brownware formulation rather than the Desert Hohokam concept is that the former is based on material culture rather than on economics and subsistence, for which we have little direct archaeological evidence. This completely misses the point that the Desert Hohokam concept includes both the material culture data and an explanation for its occurrence.

Severson (Rosenthal and others 1978: 134) concluded that Sand Papago sites may have existed in the western Papaguería as early as A.D. 1100, based on the presence of two sites (AZ Z:14:32 and Z:14:43) with Yuma II ware, Sells Plain and a few possible Tanque Verde Red-on-brown sherds. The author fails to note that "pure" Yuman and Hohokam sites, separated by an area of admixture of ceramics, have long been known for the Gila River (Fontana 1965: 96-7) and the Papaguería (Fontana 1965: 92; Ezell 1955: 17). He simply makes the assumption that the Sand Papago, to whom Papago and Yuma III sherd scatters have been attributed, also were responsible for the prehistoric pattern of mixed Yuma II and Sonoran Brownware sherds. To attribute prehistoric remains to an historically known group on the Papaguería is, at this point, an overextension of historic analogy.

In the shell analysis, Rosenthal compared the shell bracelet remains from a later Sedentary period site, AZ Z:14:22 (sic), with those from a Classic period site, AZ Z:14:33, in an attempt to test Haury's finding (1976: 313) that bracelet thickness increased from Colonial to Classic period times. Her statement that there were no significant differences between the two sites may be valid; however, her conclusion (Rosenthal and others 1978: 203) that the Quijotoa data do not support Haury's bracelet typology is overstated. Since the two sites represent only a segment of the time span with which Haury was dealing, it is not surprising that they do not exhibit the changes he defined.

Based on the analysis of the radiocarbon dates obtained from two sites with Sells phase ceramics, (AZ Z:11:5 and AZ Z:14:30), Rosenthal and others argue (1978: 214) for earlier dates, A.D. 1050-1300, for the Sells phase and would push back those for the Topawa phase to A.D. 900-1100.

An examination of Appendices V and VI of her report shows that the radiocarbon data are more ambiguous. According to the appendices, both the Laboratory of Isotope Geochemistry, Department of Geosciences, University of Arizona, and the Geochron Laboratories Division of Krueger Enterprises, Inc., were sent samples. The former laboratory obtained dendrochronologically corrected dates of A.D. 1020 ± 70 and A.D. 1080 ± 70 from two samples from unspecified proveniences at AZ Z:11:5. A similar date, A.D. 1050 ± 70, also was obtained for a hearth at AZ Z:14:30. In contrast, the sample from Hearth 1 at AZ Z:11:5 had an age of 752 ± 123 radiocarbon years (A.D. 1198 ± 123), according to Krueger Enterprises, Inc. (Rosenthal and others 1978: 279). This finding corresponds with the ceramic dates for the Sells phase. It is not clear from the report whether all samples from AZ Z:11:5 were from Hearth 1, the only feature with abundant charcoal, nor is it clear whether the techniques used by the two laboratories are comparable. Since Rosenthal does not mention, much less explain, the discrepant findings, it seems unwise to accept her suggestion that the dates for the Sells and Topawa phases be shifted.

In conclusion. it is important to note several findings of interest. These include: (1) evidence that humans have used the Quijotoa Valley, possibly since the late Pleistocene and certainly since Archaic times; (2) evidence for an increase in settlement during the Classic period, probably based on ak chin farming; and (3) evidence that the Quijotoa Valley participated in the Classic period shell trade. Despite the value of these findings, the report is flawed by poor organization, discrepancies and errors in data presentation, errors of fact, and not fully supported interpretations.

Between September 1977 and February 1978, personnel from the Cultural Resource Management Section, Arizona State Museum, surveyed locations for proposed water wells and related access roads near Kaka and Stoa Pitk. The results of the survey were summarized by McGuire and Mayro (1978). Their report provides a brief description of the environmental settings of the sites, detailed descriptions of the surface materials at each site, sketch maps, and management recommendations. They recommend that construction and access roads avoid sites entirely or that they be confined to previously disturbed areas that did not require additional data collection. The results of their survey are summarized below.

Fourteen sites were discovered. Seven of these are near Kaka, in the Kaka Valley, which ultimately drains into the Santa Rosa Basin. Seven other sites were found in the vicinity of Stoa Pitk in the Hickiwan Valley, part of the Quijotoa (San Simon) drainage basin. All but one historic Papago site, located on a ridge, are in the alluvial valley floor deposits of the two valleys.

The recorded resources document long-term human use of this area. The sites include a possible Archaic scatter, seven prehistoric (ceramic period) sherd and lithic scatters, two historic Papago sites, and a rock pile of unknown affiliation. In function, these sites range from limited activity areas to habitation villages with possible pit houses.

An examination of the raw data provided in the report yields some rather interesting findings for the sites from the Hohokam period. These sites seem to fall into two distinct categories, based on site size, kinds of ceramics, and the presence or absence of shell. The five sites under 4,000 m^2 in area were all devoid of shell; three sites were characterized by Sells Plain and Sells Red sherds and/or Tanque Verde Red-on-brown, indicating that they are Sells phase sites. Two of the sites differ somewhat; one contained Wingfield Plain sherds alone, while the other yielded Gila Plain, Sells Plain, and an unidentified red-on-buff ware. These sites contrast with the remaining five sites, characterized by a site area of over 13,000 m^2, the presence of shell, the presence of Gila Plain and/or Wingfield Plain sherds, and the absence of Sells Plain sherds. There seems to be no striking patterning in the kinds of painted wares present; the three sites with painted pottery contained Tanque Verde Red-on-brown, Sacaton and Santa Cruz red-on-buff, and Trincheras Purple-on-red. Whether this apparent clustering of sites into two categories is a matter of chance or reflects real differences in cultural affiliation, site function and period of occupation remains to be tested.

If valid, the clustering outlined above is curious in that it counters an expectation that Desert and River Hohokam sites will be found in distinctive environmental settings. Haury (1950: 547) however, notes that the geographic dividing line between the Desert and River Hohokam is blurred by the gradual merging of one into the other. Kaka and Stoa Pitk are near the divide between the Gila River drainage system and the San Simon (Quijotoa Valley) drainage system. This area might, therefore, be expected to exhibit evidence of River Hohokam expansion during the Colonial period as well as contact and exchange between the desert and river areas. The relationship between the two apparent groups of sites noted above would be a worthwhile focus of future research in the Kaka and Stoa Pitk area.

McGuire and Mayro (1978) provide detailed data for each site, which can be used for purposes of comparison with other areas. In this respect, the survey report is adequate. Summary interpretations of the sites as a group and an assessment of the significance of these resources in terms of specific problems would have enhanced the value of the report to other researchers.

Summary

To conclude this chapter, it is worthwhile to summarize what is now known about the Sells vicinity and to suggest aspects for further inquiry. Knowledge of archaeology in the vicinity of Sells remains sketchy, owing to lack of complete survey, inadequacy of recording, and problems in interpretation of small sites. Virtually nothing is known of a preceramic occupation in the project area, although reworked Archaic points have been found on one later site (AZ DD:1:21). Various reasons for the scarcity of Archaic materials may be offered. Prior to 1970 surveyors may not have recorded the low density lithic scatters from this period, because of a research focus on the Hohokam (ceramic period) chronology; sites from this period may have been buried by periodic flooding of the Sells Wash, or there may not have been a preceramic occupation of the Sells vicinity. Whether the sites are unrecorded surface scatters, buried, or simply absent is an important question that remains unresolved.

The nature of the ceramic period prehistoric occupation (Desert Hohokam) also is obscure, despite the fact that most of the recorded sites in the project area date from this period. Based on sites with decorated ceramics, it is certain that the study area was occupied by the Sells phase, but ceramics specifically from the Vamori and Topawa phases have not been identified. Many sites are characterized only by the presence of unidentified plainwares and cannot, therefore, be assigned exact dates. Whether some of these may date to the earlier ceramic phases is at present, an open question.

One of the most significant problems for the Sells area is to what extent sites in this area differ from those elsewhere in the Papaguería. There is evidence to suggest that sites in the Sells area are exceptional in their size and features. Gladwin and Gladwin (1929b: 117) noted that with the exception of sites on the Santa Cruz and near Sells, trash mounds on the Papaguería are small and uncommon. The presence of sites with a rare "Sun Temple-like enclosure" (probably a reservoir) south of Little Tucson and a site with an unusual "stadium-shaped" mound five miles southwest of Sells (Gila Pueblo site forms, on file Arizona State Museum) is further evidence that the Sells vicinity is atypical. As noted above, Jackrabbit Ruin and Valshni Village, both within 14 miles of Sells, are anomalous for the Papaguería in several respects, including their large size, the abundance of mountain sheep horn cores at Valshni Village, the presence of adobe and earth-walled enclosures at Jackrabbit Ruin, and the presence of stratified deposits at both sites. The relationships, temporal and economic, between these sites and the more common small ephemeral sherd and lithic scatters is a crucial problem, yet it has received almost no attention, largely because of the difficulties in interpreting small plainware scatters. Several sites within and near the project area contain unspecified quantities of marine shell. These sites could provide data on the role of the Baboquivari Valley in regional prehistoric systems of shell exchange, a research focus currently receiving a great deal of attention from archaeologists.

Stacy's study of the relationship between the cerros de trincheras sites and small flood plain village settlements, based on a detailed

examination of sites around Suwuk Tontk and Etoi Ki, already has shown
that sites in the vicinity of Sells can help resolve the trincheras
problem, which has long puzzled archaeologists working in the southwestern Papaguería and Sonora. An expansion of this study to include
contemporaneous sites in the project area more than 0.5 km from the
cerros de trincheras sites might help test Stacy's hypotheses that
the cerros de trincheras sites served defensive or specialized agricultural purposes for the inhabitants of the Sells phase valley floor
villages.

The question of a continuum between the Hohokam and the Pimas
and Papagos continues to be a focus of archaeological research on
the Papaguería (Haury 1950; Masse in preparation). Because of the convincing evidence that the vicinity of Sells witnessed an almost continuous occupation from the 1700s, and possibly earlier, it is highly
possible that sites in this area may help resolve the question of the
continuum.

Haury identified AZ DD:1:25 as a site dating to the period between
A.D. 1400 and 1700. Batki, or Kui Tatk, a village northwest of Sells
(outside the project area), is known from documentary sources to have
been occupied from at least the 1690s to about 1850 (Haury 1950: 19-20).
Curriden (n.d.b) identified AZ DD:1:21 as a camp site dating to A.D.
1700 ± 100 by ceramics. Despite an incomplete survey, the known
archaeological record strongly suggests a continuous sequence of
occupation, with the exception of the period between A.D. 1850 and the
founding of the Indian Oasis in the early 1900s.

One of the most pressing problems for archaeologists working in the
Papaguería is the need for new approaches to the less spectacular,
ephemeral surface scatters common to this area. Haury's telling observation (Haury 1950: 5) on the problems in interpreting the archaeological
record for the Papaguería holds especially true for small prehistoric
and historic scatters today:

> With relatively few possibilities of studying stratified remains,
> the task of reconstructing the prehistory of the Papaguería is
> a difficult one. On the whole, the archaeologist must be willing
> to expend much more time and money for what he gets than in most
> other areas. The first two seasons of intensive digging by the
> Arizona State Museum in what were considered very promising sites
> produced disappointingly small results; but these, nevertheless,
> were better than none at all.

Haury's "promising sites" were Jackrabbit Ruin and Valshni Village.
Considering this rather pessimistic evaluation of two substantial
sites, it is small wonder that the more ephemeral surface scatters
remained uninvestigated until the 1970s and that adequate field methods
still need to be developed. Stacy's (1975: 186-87) call for the

application of new field procedures and analyses to these scatters is a thorough assessment of the problem of interpreting sites on the Papaguería and is worth quoting at length:

> The scarcity of painted ceramics, a dispersed prehistoric settlement pattern, and the absence of vertical stratigraphy within sites do not facilitate use of traditional methods for chronological placement and cultural assignment of archaeological remains in the Papaguería. Application of most research methods cannot be accomplished without preliminary construction of a chronology so that sites can be separated in time. Efforts to complete a temporal framework will probably have to try use of such techniques as pollen analysis, dendrochronological studies, or archeomagnetic dating within sites, all of which are dependent upon excavated context in the Papaguería. If ceramic studies are used for chronological placement, in the absence of painted decoration, they will have to use such criteria as change in temper and vessel shape. Construction of a detailed chronology does not seem possible without excavation in a large sample of sites to provide several kinds of data which can be interpreted in chronological terms.

> Once a temporal framework exists, other studies should be possible. The absence of quantities of typeable artifacts and the lack of vertical stratigraphy in Papaguerían sites necessitates some approaches designed to extract information about man's use of an arid environment without relying strongly upon artifact analysis. A cultural ecological approach seems feasible at present, with emphasis on gathering data to study such interdependent variables as environment, subsistence, and settlement. Quantifying studies within each of these categories is desirable but may have limited usefulness for comparative purposes due to the sparse distribution of sites. A cultural ecological approach offers the advantage of utilizing such readily attainable surface information as settlement location with relation to landscape and existing natural resources, as well as information about size of sites and their proximity to one another. Excavated material could add the dimension of detailed single site studies, with artifact and feature analysis contributing toward understanding of activities at different settlement locations.

> The immediate need is for more extensive survey to establish a range of site types and their distribution on the landscape. Another need is for excavation in a selected sample of each kind of site to begin setting up a chronology for the Papaguería. With such a foundation, other studies can proceed. A cultural ecological approach as described above could prove valuable in working toward an understanding of long term cultural adaptation to an arid area.

The Sells area, with its almost continuous record of human use since the ceramic period, may be particularly useful for resolving the refractory chronological problems Stacy outlines.

Because of its long occupation, the Sells area may well have a broader importance to non-archaeologists. In view of the strong possibility of a Piman-Hohokam continuum between prehistoric and historic times, sites in the Sells area can be viewed as almost a millenium of cultural heritage for the Papago Indians.

Chapter 6

SUMMARY AND EVALUATION OF KNOWN ARCHAEOLOGICAL RESOURCES IN THE PROJECT AREA

In this chapter the archaeological resources within the project area are summarized, and archaeologically sensitive areas are identified. The significance of these resources is evaluated on the basis of the gaps in our understanding of the past on the Papaguería and of the potential of the resources to resolve these problems.

The specific site data on which this chapter is based are summarized in Tables 6 through 8. Readers wishing more detailed information should refer to the tables.

Summary of Known Cultural Resources

Surveys between 1928 and the present have resulted in the discovery of 18 archaeological sites within project boundaries. Tables in this chapter were compiled from data recorded on the original site cards and survey forms, maps and in some cases, field notes on file at ASM and WAC. Table 6 indicates the cultural and temporal affiliations, size, setting and known disturbance for each site. Table 7 provides more detailed information on artifact assemblages, features and cultural deposition for each site. Table 8 summarizes archival information (e.g., recording institution, data and location of original site records, location of collections, the kinds of data recovery, if any, and relevant references). Appendix A, containing legal descriptions of site locations, and Figure 2, showing site locations and surveyed areas, are deleted from most copies of this report in order to protect the archaeological resources.

At the outset, it should be emphasized that the data available for the project area are incomplete. The 18 known archaeological sites within the project boundaries do not in any way represent a complete inventory of the cultural resources in the project area. Prior to 1970, survey coverage was confined to readily accessible areas in which sites were expected. Later, surveys were limited to intensive inspections of small areas. It is noteworthy that cultural materials of varying degrees of significance and integrity (but not necessarily of site status) have been found in almost every surveyed area within project boundaries. It is likely, therefore, that many more unrecorded sites exist in the project area.

It should be noted that the relatively high expected site density within the project area is not an isolated phenomenon, but part of a general pattern throughout at least the area encompassed by the U.S.G.S. Sells 15 minute Quadrangle. Gila Pueblo, ASM and WAC recorded some 55 additional archaeological sites outside the project area in the quadrangle. These include Jackrabbit Ruin and Valshni Village, the type sites for the Desert Hohokam sequence. Although the resources outside the project area do not receive detailed treatment in this report, it is clear from the total number of known sites in the U.S.G.S. Sells 15 minute Quadrangle that the Sells area has been an important focus of human occupation.

The general trends identified below are based on incomplete records for the 18 known sites within the project area. As noted in Chapter 5, research purposes and procedures have changed since the first surveys in the project area, so that data for the known sites are biased or uneven. Early surveys, which were biased toward the larger, denser ceramic period scatters with trash mounds, may have left plainware and nonceramic scatters unrecorded. Survey forms from the pre-World War II research period often contain little or no information on lithic assemblages, artifact concentrations, and features other than trash mounds. We have no data on several categories of evidence for a number of sites, as a review of Tables 6 and 7 will show. Exact locations for the Gila Pueblo sites are unknown; we can identify only general areas in which the sites may be located. Data from the 1970s research period also are incomplete for several sites. At least three sites cannot be fully evaluated since they are only partially exposed by soil disturbance and have not received further study or testing. As a result of incomplete survey coverage and site records, the characteristics of the archaeological resources below should be viewed only as a general indication of the nature of the resources one may expect to find in the project area. It is expected that future resources will expand and revise this interpretation.

With the exception of a lithic scatter (camp or quarry area) and a site recorded as a "sherd area," all known sites in the project area are sherd and lithic scatters. These range from small sparse scatters 10 m in diameter to large dense sites with a variety of surface features covering an area of 1500 m by 2500 m. Of the 16 sites whose dimensions are known, five are under 600 m^2 in area, four range between 1,000 m^2 and 6,000 m^2, five are between 10,000 m^2 and "several acres," and two cover more than 100,000 m^2. Although this apparent clustering is based on a small number of sites, it suggests that a full range of archaeological manifestations, from limited activity areas to large villages inhabited either by a large group of people or over an extended period of time, are represented in the archaeological record. More exact functions cannot be assigned to these sites without extensive data recovery and detailed artifact analyses.

The exact cultural and temporal affiliations of several of the sites are in question because of incomplete survey data or a lack

of diagnostic lithic and ceramic material. Nonetheless, it is clear
from Table 6 that all periods following A.D. 800 (the approximate date
for the appearance of Vamori phase sites in the Papaguería) are represented in the project area. Sites within project boundaries include
Desert Hohokam (A.D. 800-1400) manifestations, post-Classic period
(A.D. 1400-1700)scatters, and historic Papago (A.D. 1700-1850)
sites. Since the modern town of Sells was established in the early 20th
century, sites in the project area have the potential to provide an
almost continuous record of the last 1,200 years.

Although artifact assemblages of the known sites have been
inconsistently recorded, it is evident from Table 7 that sherd
and lithic scatters share several characteristics in lithic and
ceramic features. The recorded chipped stone assemblages consist
primarily of flakes, shatter and cores, with few or no formal tools.
Raw materials for chipped stone are predominantly igneous materials,
although cryptocrystalline materials such as agate and jasper also
occur. Sources for these raw materials have been identified in the
Artesa Mountains south of Sells, and these show definite evidence of
quarrying activities during at least the Sells phase. Generalizations
cannot be made at this time from the limited data on ground stone
assemblages.

Ceramic assemblages are consistently dominated by plainware
pottery. Redware or decorated red-on-brown sherds are rare or absent.

Many sites exhibit no surface features. On the larger sites,
a few widely dispersed trash mound and artifact concentrations are the
most common features visible on the surface. Hearths, charcos (reservoirs), cremations, bedrock mortars and petroglyphs, though present
in the project area, are rare. Distinct house remains have not been
discerned on the surface of any site in the project area. Trincheras-
like architecture has been noted on only one site within project boundaries.
More trincheras features are likely to be found on hill tops, a setting
which has received almost no survey within the project area.

Comparatively little is known of the nature of materials below
the surface scatters. Testing on sites along PIR 24 and at AZ DD:1:21
indicates that cultural deposits often are shallow; however, this
finding is inconclusive because subsurface investigations usually were
limited to fewer than six test pits per site. Stacy (1975: 184) notes
that elsewhere on the Papaguería more subsurface features were discovered
in blade cuts for roads than in her test pit excavations. This suggests
that limited test pit excavations may not be effective for locating
buried features. Extensive trenching and soil stripping, rather than
small test pits, may be more appropriate for determining whether surface
sites have cultural deposition or subsurface features.

In addition to exhibiting common characteristics in artifact
assemblages and features, the 18 archaeological sites within the project
area also show patterns in location:

1) Sites buried by alluvium have been discovered within 0.2 mile of Sells Wash;
2) Surface sherd and lithic scatters occur along Sells Wash; and,
3) Surface sherd and lithic scatters occur at the base of Etoi Ki.

Sites outside the project area indicate that additional patterns may be expected in the project area:

1) Cerros de trincheras sites should occur on hill tops south and east of Sells;
2) Lithic scatters (quarries) should be found at outcrops of suitable fine-grained or glassy raw material on, or at the bases of mountains south and east of Sells.

Site density between Etoi Ki and Sells Wash cannot be accurately predicted, owing to inadequate survey coverage. One site occurs in this setting, an area drained by numerous shallow washes. Because of its suitability for ak chin farming, small prehistoric and historic summer farming villages should be expected in this setting.

To some extent, these patterns in site locations reflect differential survey coverage within the project area. Nonetheless, preliminary survey data from other valleys on the Papaguería tend to confirm the validity of this patterning. According to Stacy (1975: 185), Sells phase sites were equally divided between locations on the alluvial valley floor and near hills or series of hills, regardless of site function. Those on the valley floor were consistently found between two large washes within 0.5 mile of one or the other, or within 0.5 mile of the bank of a single major wash in an area where the streambed formed a dendritic pattern. The Sells Wash is an example of just such a major wash. A similar selection of valley floor and hill settings for summer field and winter well villages is known for 19th century Papago sites and presumably existed for earlier Papago villages, as well.

Archaeologically Sensitive Areas

Combining site locations within the project area with general survey data from the Papaguería, the following locales in the project area appear to have a high potential for archaeological sites:

1) an area 0.5 mile wide on either side of Sells Wash;
2) the area between Sells Wash and Little Tucson Wash, within 0.5 mile of either wash;
3) the bases of isolated hills near Etoi Ki;
4) the base of the Artesa Mountains; and,
5) isolated hill tops and mountain zones.

Cerros de trincheras sites and lithic quarries are expected to be confined to Area 5, which will not be affected by planned modifications of the sewer system at this time (see Chapter 7). Areas 1 through 4 are expected to have sherd and lithic scatters of varying density representing a range of functions from limited activity areas to large habitation sites. Areas 1 and 2 also have a high potential for buried sites, since they are subject to periodic flooding (U.S. Army Corps of Engineers 1976). The presence of at least three buried sites in Area 1 strongly supports the designation of this setting as an archaeologically sensitive area. In addition to the areas specified above, undisturbed areas north of Sells Wash and any areas subject to alluviation may contain evidence of past cultures.

Significance of Recorded Resources in the Project Area

The remainder of this chapter consists of an evaluation of the archaeological significance of resources in the project area based on a consideration of gaps in our understanding of the prehistory and history of the Papaguería and on the potential of project area resources to resolve these problems. Gaps in knowledge that require further research are identified in Chapter 5 and are briefly reviewed here. Next, the research potential of the known sites within the project area is identified in terms of these gaps. Last, the significance of resources within the project area is outlined. The ethnic significance of these resources for The Papago Tribe is not evaluated in detail, since it is felt that The Papago Tribe is better able to make a judgement on this matter.

Chapter 4 shows that during the Desert Hohokam period, the Papaguería was a marginal area where inhabitants practiced a mixed economy based on the collection of wild plants and animal resources and ak chin agriculture. While the central zone of the Papaguería exhibits distinctive characteristics and history, owing to adaptations to a hostile marginal environment, the Desert Hohokam shared many traits with adjacent regions. For the most part, these ties have been defined on the basis of the presence of trade goods (especially ceramics) from the Tucson and Gila basins, Sonora and, to a lesser degree, the lower Colorado region. More recently, shell trade routes have become a focus of research in the Papaguería. Despite this recent interest, very little is known in detail of the exact economic or political relationships between regions. It has been theorized (Haury 1950), that colonists from the Gila Basin initiated the ceramic period settlement in the Papaguería. How, or whether, this area functioned as part of a larger Hohokam region has not been determined. Similarly, strong ceramic affinities between the Papaguería and the Tucson Basin have been noted but not fully explored. Lack of data and problems in chronology hamper our understanding of regional relationships between the Papaguería and Sonora and the lower Colorado Valley. The nature of trade and other economic ties, how they were operated and maintained, their integrative functions and what was traded are all aspects that require further research. The Sells area, with evidence for ties with the Gila-Salt and Tucson basins, Sonora and the lower Colorado region, may help resolve this problem.

Chapter 5 concludes with a brief summary of unresolved problems in the archaeology of the Sells area in particular and the Papaguería in general. The unexplained absence of Archaic period sites within the project area is noted and merits further investigation. Many aspects of the ceramic period (Desert Hohokam) sequence require further study. The lack of data on pre-Sells (Vamori and Topawa) phases and the need to develop a chronological framework for plainwares are identified. It is suggested that the Sells area is somewhat anomalous for the Papaguería, in terms of the presence of large village sites with stratified trash mounds, such as Jackrabbit Ruin and Valshni Village. Rather rare features, and artifacts, such as "stadium-shaped mounds" and "Sun Temple-like enclosures" (Gila Pueblo sites), earthen and adobe enclosures (Jackrabbit Ruin), and abundant mountain sheep horns (Valshni Village) have been observed in the Sells vicinity.

An explanation for such a variety of rather unusual features around Sells has not been developed. Relationships between sites in the Baboquivari Valley and other areas have not been investigated. The relationships among small plainware scatters and the larger, more varied sites in the Baboquivari Valley will remain obscure until we have a much clearer understanding of the chronological placement and function(s) of the ephemeral plainware scatters. Detailed studies of such sites have not been undertaken in the project area. It is known from two sites within the project area, and from Jackrabbit Ruin and Valshni Village, that the Baboquivari Valley participated to some degree in prehistoric shell trade networks, but almost nothing is known of the specifics of this exchange for this valley.

Very little is known of the post-Classic period between A.D. 1400 and 1700 throughout southern Arizona, and the question of a Hohokam-Piman continuum remains unresolved. One known site in the project area was occupied during this period.

Although historical sources from the period between A.D. 1700 and 1850 are fairly informative, the archaeology of the historic Papago period has received little study. The Baboquivari and Comobabi mountains and their extensions were some of the richer gathering grounds in the central zone of the Papaguería (Hackenberg 1964: IV-139) as well as important mining districts during the historic period. Historic Papago sites in mountainous areas and on the valley floor may help elucidate Papago subsistence practices, the degree of participation in the non-Indian economy, and acculturation processes for this period.

The need for the development of new field methods and analytical procedures, particularly for ephemeral surface scatters, is identified in Chapter 5. The only major excavations in the Sells area were undertaken in the 1930s and 1940s. Excavations since that time have been confined to more limited test excavations. Current techniques of excavation, including the use of natural stratigraphy, statistical analyses of artifactual material, pollen and macrobotanical analyses, and archaeomagnetic and radiocarbon dating techniques, have not been applied to sites in the project area. With these techniques, much more could be learned from excavation of sites with cultural deposition than was possible in the past.

Sites in the project area have a high potential to contribute to the resolution of the specific problems noted above. As documented in this report, sites in the project area represent an almost continuous record for the last 1,200 years. This unusually complete record indicates that long term processes of change, as well as the wide range of specific problems noted above, can be addressed in the project area.

Because of the presence of stratified deposits in the project area and the existence of comparative data from nearby excavated villages, sites in the project area can be studied to clarify the nature of prehistoric settlement in the Baboquivari Valley and to develop a better chronological framework for Desert Hohokam sites. As a result of the excavation of Jackrabbit Ruin and Valshni Village, we have some understanding of the large village component of the Desert Hohokam subsistence-settlement pattern in the Baboquivari Valley; contemporaneous sites in the project area may provide data on the remaining components of that system: collecting and processing sites, farming villages, quarry areas, and "defensive" features (cerros de trincheras architecture). Careful excavation of stratified deposits and detailed attribute analyses of the recovered plainware ceramics could be an effective means of developing a reliable chronological framework, into which plainware surface scatters could then be placed. Because of their general scarcity in the Papaguería, the stratified deposits in the project area are all the more important for future studies in Papaguería prehistory.

Sites in the project area appear to bridge the gap between A.D. 1400 and 1700 in the archaeological record. Thus, the project area may be uniquely suited to answering the question of a Hohokam-Piman continuum. This long-standing problem warrants much further study.

Historic Papago sites have been recorded within and adjacent to the project area. Data from such sites can supplement and verify the documentary sources on historic Papago lifeways.

Although one site, AZ DD:1:34, has been found worthy of nomination to the National Register of Historic Places (D. Brown 1976), the archaeological significance of each previously recorded site in the project area cannot be determined on the basis of current knowledge. A reliable determination of significance would depend on, among other factors, a consideration of the surface characteristics of each site, the presence of subsurface deposits, the present degree of disturbance, and the effects of disturbance on the overall integrity of the resource. Thus, on-site inspection and, in some cases, test excavations would be necessary to accurately assess the research value of each site.

Although the available data are not sufficient to specify the exact significance of each known resource within the project area, a general statement of significance is possible. It has been shown that in terms of site functions and periods of occupation, the project area contains a wide range of archaeological resources. The long, almost continuous record of occupation and the presence of stratified deposits give the project area a high potential for important contributions to our knowledge of the Baboquivari Valley and its past relationships to other areas of the Papaguería and adjacent regions. Studies in the project area also have the potential to contribute to the development of new, more appropriate archaeological methods and theories for ephemeral surface scatters commonly found in the Papaguería. Because of these considerations, the previously recorded archaeological resources in the project area are judged to be highly significant as segments of social systems operating in the past. Because of the likelihood of additional unrecorded resources in the project area, other sites may also be judged at a later date to be highly significant archaeological resources.

The strong possibility of a Hohokam-Piman continuum and the long record of occupation in and near Sells have received emphasis in this report. In view of these factors, prehistoric and post-Classic sites, as well as historic Papago manifestations, may have significance to The Papago Tribe as part of its cultural heritage. It is felt that any evaluation of the ethnic significance of the resources in the project area is beyond the scope of this assessment.

113

Table 6. Basic Site Data: Cultural/Temporal Affiliation, Site Type, Size, Setting, Disturbance and Comments

Site Number	Cultural Affiliation/Temporal Placement	Site Type	Site Dimension	Site Area (m²)	Site Setting	Known Disturbance
GP Sonora D:1:1	Aboriginal/Unknown	Camp, quarry	Recorded as "200 ft"	?	Hills	**
GP Sonora D:1:2	Prehistoric ?/A.D. 800 to 1400 ?	Village	200 ft by 300 ft	5,574	Valley floor	**
GP Sonora D:1:6	Desert Hohokam; Classic period/A.D. 1400	Village	100 ft N-S by 200 ft E-W	1,858	Valley floor	**
GP Sonora D:1:7/8	Desert Hohokam; Classic period/A.D. 1400	Village	"Perhaps 800 ft by 250 ft"	18,581	Valley floor	Disturbed by old Route 86 from Sells to Ajo.
AZ DD:1:10	Papago/pre-1830 (?)	"Sherd area"	"Several acres"	*	Mesquite flat in foothills	**
AZ DD:1:21	Papago/A.D. 1700⁺-100	Camp	200 m by 100 m	20,000	Valley floor	Site slated for destruction by Health Complex.
AZ DD:1:22	Desert Hohokam; Sells phase/A.D. 1250-1400	Village	"Several acres"	*	Valley floor	**
AZ DD:1:25	Post-Classic w/lesser amounts of Sells phase and modern Papago materials/A.D. 1400-1700; A.D. 1250-1400; post 1700?	Village & charco	125 m by 150 m	18,750	Valley floor	**
AZ DD:1:29	Desert Hohokam; Unknown phase/A.D. 800-1400	Village	50 m by 50 m	2,500	Valley floor	Some disturbance likely; extent unknown.
AZ DD:1:33	Desert Hohokam; Sells phase/A.D. 1250-1400	Village	300 m by 600 m	180,000	Valley floor	Minor sheet wash disturbance.
AZ DD:1:34	Desert Hohokam; Sells phase/A.D. 1250-1400	Village	1500 m by 2500 m	3,750,000	Valley floor	Construction of new rodeo grounds, Route 86, sheet wash disturbance.
PIR 119	Unknown/Unknown	Unknown	**	**	Valley floor	Disturbed by previous road construction.
PIR 3	Desert Hohokam; Sells phase (?)/A.D. 1250-1400(?)	Unknown	25 ft by 25 ft	58	Valley floor	Disturbed by previous road and dike construction.

Table 6 (continued)

Site Number	Cultural Affiliation/Temporal Placement	Site Type	Site Dimension	Site Area (m²)	Site Setting	Known Disturbance
PIR 4	Desert Hohokam; Unknown phase/A.D. 800-1400	Unknown	75 ft by 50 ft	348	Valley floor	Ground surface disturbed by road and dike construction.
AZ DD:1:42	Desert Hohokam/Unknown phase/A.D. 800-1400	Unknown	20 m by 30 m	600	Valley floor	Ground surface disturbed by road and dike construction.
AZ DD:1:45	Desert Hohokam; Sells phase (?)/A.D. 1250-1400(?)	Camp? Village?	70 m by 30 m	2,100	Valley floor	Eroded near Sells Wash; previously disturbed by road and dike construction.
Rodeo 1	Unknown	Unknown	10 m by 10 m	100	Valley floor	Site is disturbed by parking lot; heavy use in recent times.
Rodeo 2	Unknown	Unknown	20 m by 20 m	400	Valley floor	Disturbed by fence, dirt road; heavy use in recent times.

* 1 acre equals 4049 m²; sites several acres in area are probably between 10,000 m² and 100,000 m².
** signifies no recorded information.

Table 7. Basic Site Data: Artifacts, Features & Cultural Deposits

Site Number	Artifacts			Features						Sub-Surface Deposits	Comments
	Pottery	Lithics	Other	Trash Mounds	Concentrations	Hearths	Houses	"Stony spots"	Other		
GP Sonora D:1:1	sparse, Papago?	no ground stone	no	no	no	no	no	no	no	no	Gila Pueblo records this as a possible quarry but provides no data on lithics. Raw materials are agates, quartz.
GP Sonora D:1:2	Polished redwares present, no polychromes	present	--	yes, 2	--	--	no	yes, 5-6	--	possible	Deposition not greater than 30 cm according to recorder.
GP Sonora D:1:6	present	--	yes, shell	yes, 1	--	--	no	--	yes	possible	Deposition of 30 cm possible according to recorder.
GP Sonora D:1:7/8	present	present, includes metates	--	yes, 4	--	--	--	--	--	yes	Trash mounds are from 14" to 26" high and 20 to 30 feet wide; deposition of at least 60 cm possible.
AZ DD:1:10	Historic Papago	--	--	--	--	--	--	--	--	no	Absence of china and iron may put this back 100 or more years according to recorder. Painted pottery is very rare.
AZ DD:1:21	Historic Papago	cores, flakes, shatter, scraping tools	absent	absent	yes	yes	no	no	no	no	Area of site within Health Complex; has been collected & tested.

Table 7 (continued)

Site Number	Artifacts			Features							Comments
	Pottery	Lithics	Other	Trash Mounds	Concen- trations	Hearths	Houses	"Stony spots"	Other	Sub- Surface Deposits	
AZ DD:1:22	Sells Red, Un- identi- fied red/ brown & plain	stone blades, manos, hoes	--	yes	--	--	--	--	no	50 cm or more	Has deposits of at least "0.5" (unit of measure probably meters).
AZ DD:1:25	Uniden- tified red, plain, red/ brown	--	--	--	--	--	--	--	"charco"	1.0 m or more	Range of very abundant pottery; much is not Sells phase or post- A.D. 1750. Haury (recorder) suggests much may be A.D. 1450- 1700.
AZ DD:1:29	red/ brown, plain, red	mano frag- ments, no other data	shell, recent Papago trash	--	--	--	--	--	pot crema- tion	yes	Deposits approximately 75 cm deep. Discovered during local dirt-moving operation.
AZ DD:1:33	Sells plain, Tanque Verde red/ brown, Sells red	primary flakes, cores, manos metates	--	2	yes	no	no	no	no	yes, depth unknown	Deposition unknown.
AZ DD:1:34	Sells plain & red, Tanque Verde Red/ brown	primary flakes, cores, choppers	no	4	yes	no	no	no	Pe, BM, TF	yes, depth unknown	Site possesses 3 distinct activity areas: 1) lithic reduction area, 2) sherds and bedrock mortars, and 3) 4 trash mounds.

Table 7 (continued)

Site Number	Artifacts			Features							Comments
	Pottery	Lithics	Other	Trash Mounds	Concen-trations	Hearths	Houses	"Stony spots"	Other	Sub-Surface Deposits	
PIR 119	Uniden-tified plain	present	fire-cracked rock	--	--	--	--	--	--	--	Area subject to alluviation by Sells Wash.
PIR 3	pre-his-toric plains, Tanque Verde red/brown	flakes	no	no	no	no	no	no	no	probable	Area subject to alluviation by Sells Wash. Site form indicates there is no evidence of cultural deposits, however materials were found only where surface is dis-turbed so deposits possible.
PIR 4	pre-historic plains	flakes, cores, tools, manos	no	no	no	no	no	no	no	yes	Area subject to alluviation by Sells Wash. Cultural materials occur only where surface is dis-turbed. Site covered by more than 30 cm of alluvium.
AZ DD:1:42	pre-historic plains	flakes, core, mano	no	no	no	no	no	no	no	yes	Area subject to alluviation. Cultural materials occur only where surface is disturbed. Site covered by more than 30 cm of alluvium.
AZ DD:1:45	pre-historic plains, Tanque Verde Red/brown	flakes, cores, tools, manos, metates	no	no	yes	(recent) yes	no	no	no	yes	Very sparse material found below surface in test pits in concentrations; pits excavated to between 2'5" and 3'4"; no features found. Road rerouted to avoid site.

Table 7 (continued)

Site Number	Artifacts			Features						Comments
	Pottery	Lithics	Other	Trash Mounds	Concen-trations	Hearths	Houses	"Stony spots"	Other	Sub-Surface Deposits	
Rodeo 1	Polished red	a few flakes	no	no	no	no	no	no	no	--	Site is heavily disturbed by recent activities. Site has not been tested for sub-surface deposits.
Rodeo 2	uniden-tified plain	1 core, col-lected; 2 flakes, 1 col-lected	no	no	no	no	no	no	no	--	Site is heavily disturbed by recent activities. Site has not been tested for sub-surface deposits.

-- signifies no data available
Pe Petroglyphs
BM Bedrock Mortars
TF Trincheras features

Table 6. Site Data: Recording Institution, Date and Location of Original Site Records, Survey and Data Recovery Collections, and Publications

Site Number	Recorded by	Date Recorded	Location of Original Site Records	Survey Collections	Systematic Collection (C) Excavation (E) Testing (T)	Publications
GP Sonora D:1:1	Gila Pueblo	1928	ASM	Yes, ASM	No	Gladwin and Gladwin 1929b
GP Sonora D:1:2	Gila Pueblo	1928	ASM	Yes, ASM	No	As above
GP Sonora D:1:6	Gila Pueblo	1928	ASM	Yes, ASM	No	As above
GP Sonora D:1:7/8	Gila Pueblo	1929	ASM	Yes, ASM	No	As above
AZ DD:1:10	ASM*	1938	ASM	No	No	No
AZ DD:1:21	ASM	1976	ASM	Yes, ASM	C & T	Teague 1976 Curriden n.d.b
AZ DD:1:22	ASM	1939	ASM	Yes, ASM	No	No
AZ DD:1:25	ASM	1940	ASM	Yes, ASM	No	No
AZ DD:1:29	ASM	1962	ASM	Yes, ASM	No	No
AZ DD:1:33	ASM	1974	ASM	No	No	Stacy (1974)
AZ DD:1:34	ASM	1974	ASM	No	No	Stacy (1974)
PIR 119	WAC*	1973	WAC	**	No	Stacy (1973)
PIR 3	WAC	1973	WAC	Yes, WAC	No	No
PIR 4	WAC	1973	WAC	Yes, WAC	No	No
AZ DD:1:42	WAC	1973	WAC, ASM	Yes, WAC	No	No
AZ DD:1:45	WAC	1973	WAC, ASM	Yes, WAC	T:5 or 6, 5' by 5', No test pits	No
Rodeo 1	WAC	1974	WAC	Yes, WAC	No	No
Rodeo 2	WAC	1974	WAC	Yes, WAC	No	No

*ASM = Arizona State Museum
WAC = Western Archeological Center
**No Information Available.

CHAPTER 7

IMPACTS AND RECOMMENDATIONS

The following discussion of impacts and recommendations is divided into three sections. The first section identifies the probable impacts of various existing natural and human activities upon cultural resources in the project area. The second section, the major portion of this chapter, is a discussion of proposed modifications in the Sells wastewater facilities, and their projected effects on cultural resources. This section also contains management recommendations for specific modifications in the sewer system. The last section provides general, long term management recommendations for the project area.

Before discussing existing disturbance in the project area a brief statement on the methods used to determine impact and to develop archaeological recommendations is in order. The assessment of the effects of existing disturbances is based on general considerations of topography, observations by archaeologists on local soil erosion and deposition, and a visit to the project area by Sharon S. Debowski, Cultural Resource Management Section (CRMS), project director for the Sells assessment and Carol A. Coe, CRMS archaeologist. The effects of proposed modifications are identified on the basis of the evidence above, in conjunction with a consideration of expected construction activities.

Existing Disturbance

The major sources of natural disturbance of archaeological resources in the project area are soil erosion and deposition. A study of the Sells and Little Tucson washes in the vicinity of Sells by the U.S. Army Corps of Engineers (1976) indicates areas subject to sheet wash flooding during 100 and 500 year floods. One site in this flood area, AZ DD:1:21, is known to have been affected by sheet wash erosion (Curriden n.d.b). It is likely that less severe but more widespread sheet wash erosion and deposition have affected other resources both within and outside the 500 year flood limit. Stacy (1974) indicates that alluviation may have buried materials around Etoi Ki. The degree of adverse effects on a specific site will depend not only on the severity and extent of sheet wash, but also on the nature of the resource. Thus, the displacement of surface artifacts by sheet wash may prohibit the delineation of specific activity areas within a surface site, thereby substantially altering its research potential. The same degree of soil (and artifact) disturbance may destroy only a fraction of the potential information obtainable from a stratified site with subsurface cultural deposits. On-site inspection is needed to evaluate the effects of sheet wash erosion and deposition on individual resources in the project area.

Channel cutting and alluviation in and adjacent to Sells Wash and Little Tucson Wash may have removed or buried cultural materials, leaving few cultural traces visible on the surface. At least three sites north of Sells Wash (PIR 3, PIR 4, AZ DD:1:42) were detected only in areas where 30 cm of alluvium were removed during construction. A fourth site (AZ DD:1:29) also may have been visible only when earth moving operations exposed it, but this is not clear from the site card on file at ASM. Whether natural processes will wash away all traces of a site or bury and preserve it depends on numerous local factors. Systematic testing in areas subject to alluviation and monitoring of earth moving operations are the only effective means of determining whether buried cultural resources are present.

Minor disturbance of cultural resources may be expected as a result of cattle grazing and random surface collecting. Cattle can break or damage surface artifacts or disturb their original distribution. Collecting may remove certain categories of artifacts, such as projectile points and ground stone, from site surfaces, leaving a skewed record of activities represented at the site. These activities are not expected to have substantially diminished the research potential of sites in the project area.

Debowski and Coe visited the project area on October 11, 1978. They noted heavy ground disturbance in Sells itself and relatively little land modification outside Sells. Building, road and utilities construction and related land moving operations have altered the original ground surface in much of Sells. It is expected that intact surface sites will not be found in such highly disturbed areas, although isolated artifacts may still be present.

Much of the project area shows little evidence of recent human disturbance. North of Sells Wash a series of dikes and ponds have been built for irrigation and water storage. The total area affected by these devices and related agricultural activities is comparatively small. While some sites may have been altered by these activities, the adverse effects on the archaeological record as a whole are not believed to be extensive.

In summary, sheet wash erosion and minor land disturbances are expected to have had the greatest effects on sites outside Sells within the project area. It is believed that the total archaeological record has not been substantially altered or its integrity diminished by these natural forces and human activities. Within Sells, existing surface disturbance from a variety of construction activities is extensive. As a result, surface sites are not likely to be found in disturbed areas. Despite extensive surface disturbance, the research potential within Sells remains high. As Chapter 6 documents, most of Sells is in an archaeological sensitive area where buried sites may be expected. Surface scatters with cultural deposits and sites buried by alluvium may still provide abundant data, although the ground surface has been disturbed.

Proposed Improvements in the Papago Tribal Utilities Authority (P.T.U.A.) Wastewater Facilities: Modifications, Probable Effects, and Management Recommendations

Several improvements of the secondary sewage treatment system have been proposed for the town of Sells (STRAAM Engineers, Inc. 1978). These include (1) the replacement of a 5,300-foot segment of an 8-inch-diameter pipe from Manhole A-6 to Manhole D-0 and from Manhole D-0 to Manhole D-13 with a 10-inch-diameter pipeline. (This 5,300-foot segment corresponds to the line between Manhole 315 and Manhole 341 on maps supplied by Papago Tribal Utilities Authority); (2) relaying the 10-inch-pipe from Manhole A-1 to the sewage ponds; (3) improvement of existing sewage ponds (hereafter called "cells") west of the town; and (4) retrofitting of the existing lift station. In addition, sewer lines from the houses to the existing sewer line will be added to the housing subdivision on the east side of town.

All of these improvements lie within 0.5 mile of either Sells Wash or Little Tucson Wash, the areas with a high potential for surface and buried sites identified in Chapter 6. The recommendations that follow include archaeological monitoring where the present ground surface has been modified in historic times ("disturbed" areas) and intensive survey and monitoring in undisturbed areas. Specific recommendations have been developed for the areas to be affected by pipeline improvement, improvement of the cells, construction of new sewer lines, and retrofitting the existing lift station. These recommendations are based on a consideration of the following factors:

1. the kinds of soil disturbance expected by construction,
2. the extent of prior archaeological survey in each area,
3. the existence of known sites near the improvements,
4. the potential for sites, and
5. the degree of recent soil disturbance in each area.

These recommendations are summarized in Table 9 and are discussed in detail below.

Table 9. Summary of Recommendations

	Proposed Improvement	Previous Survey	Known Sites	Recommendations
A.	Replacement of 8-inch pipe with 10-inch pipe, Manhole A-6 to D-0 and D-0 to D-13	rodeo grounds preschool complex new tribal offices	Rodeo 1 and Rodeo 2; approximately 300 to 600 feet north of line	Monitor backhoe trenches during construction.
B.	1) Modifications of sewage "cells" (System A) and improvement of pipeline from Manhole A-1 to sewage cells	extent of previous survey unknown	AZ DD:1:22 within 500 feet of existing cells	Prior to construction, survey of locations for new cells, pipelines, buildings and any additional area to be affected by construction. Monitoring of same during earth-moving operations.
	2) Application of effluent to acreage near cells (Alternate System D)	as above	as above	Survey of acreage to be affected by irrigation construction if System D is selected; further recommendations or additional work are to be based on survey findings.
C.	"Feeder" sewer lines 1) Subdivision parcel	Doelle and Brew (1976)	Sparse scatter of prehistoric and historic artifacts; not given site status.	Monitor backhoe trenches from houses to existing pipeline.
	2) Water and erosion control modifications south of subdivision parcel	none	none	Survey area subject to land modification prior to construction. Monitor construction.
	3) Feeder sewer lines from isolated housing lots	11 lots unsurveyed; See Appendix C for unsurveyed lots	none	Examine unsurveyed lots. Monitor backhoe trenches from houses to main sewer lines.

Replacement of Existing Pipeline from Manhole A-6 to Manhole D-0
and from Manhole D-0 to Manhole D-13

In the draft report by STRAAM Engineers, Inc. (1978), this replacement
segment ran from Manhole A-6 to Manhole D-0 and from Manhole D-0 to D-11.
The segment has since been extended to Manhole D-13, according to Henry
G. Atha, P.T.U.A. According to Atha, Manholes A-6, D-0 and D-13 are those
designated as Manholes 315, 319 and 341 on the Papago Indian Reservation
community land ownership and utilities maps provided by P.T.U.A. to ASM.

The replacement segment from Manhole A-6 to Manhole D-0 and from
Manhole D-0 to D-13 is approximately 5,300 feet long. In this area a
new 10-inch-diameter pipeline will be placed next to the existing 8-inch-
pipeline, leaving the existing line intact. Ground disturbance that may
affect archaeological resources will consist primarily of a backhoe
trench approximately 3 feet wide and a minimum of 4 feet deep. Some
disturbance of the present ground surface also is likely, but because of
the degree of previous soil disturbance, this is expected to have little
additional affect on archaeological materials on the surface.

With the exception of the rodeo grounds, the preschool complex and
the new tribal buildings, the area to be affected by the replacement of
the pipeline has not been surveyed for archaeological resources. Two
archaeological sites, Rodeo 1 and Rodeo 2, have been discovered in the
former Rodeo Ground approximately 300 to 600 feet north of the existing
pipeline. These consist of small (under 20 m in diameter) sparse sherd
and lithic scatters, which have not been tested for subsurface materials.
Both scatters are in a disturbed context and will not be directly
affected by replacement of the existing pipeline; however, because the
area is one where buried cultural materials are likely, it is possible
that additional buried materials may extend into the pipeline area. As
noted, this segment of pipeline exists in an archaeologically sensitive
area where buried sites may be expected.

As noted, in October 1978 the area in which the pipeline will be
replaced was briefly inspected by Debowski and Coe. Based on the heavy
disturbance by building and roads, it is unlikely that intact surface
sites now exist in this area; therefore further archaeological survey
is not recommneded. It is recommended that the backhoe trench for the
new pipeline be inspected for cultural materials and features by an
archaeological monitor. Plans for mitigating the adverse effects of
construction would then be developed should any significant cultural
resources be discovered during monitoring.

Expansion or Improvement of Sewage Ponds (Cells) and Pipeline
from Manhole A-1 to Cells

The draft report of the facility plan for Sells (STRAAM Engineers,
Inc. 1978) described four improvement alternatives, Systems A through D,

for the effluent cells. All four include relaying the 10-inch-diameter pipe from Manhole A-1 to the cells. System A calls for the construction of two new cells on the south and west sides of existing Cell 2 and the addition of new piping and measuring equipment. Alternate plans (Systems B through D) call for chlorinating and/or aerating the effluent and applying it to 20 to 30 acres of land near the cells for irrigation. The 30 to 40 feet of pipeline to be relaid between Manhole A-1 and the junction box at the cells will be affected primarily by trenching operations. The proposed additions to the cells involve earth moving operations adjacent to existing Cells 2 and 3. The alternate plan for chlorination facilities (System B) calls for lining the existing cells and constructing new metering and chlorination facilities. This alternative is expected to involve little new ground disturbance. A second alternative to constructing new cells is the construction of aeration and chlorination facilities (System C). In addition to lining the cells for chlorination, this construction includes deepening Cell 2. A third alternative, System D, consists of the use of the effluent from either System B or System C for irrigating several acres of land near the lagoons. In addition to the land modifications above, System D would involve preparation of the land for irrigation by removing vegetation and leveling the land.

The area around the cells has not beeen systematically surveyed. A single site, AZ DD:1:22, recorded in 1939, is in the vicinity of the cells. Based on a comparison of maps in the U.S. Army Corps of Engineers report (1976) with U.S.G.S. maps on file at ASM, the existing cells appear to be within 500 feet north of AZ DD:1:22. At the time it was discovered, the site was characterized as a Sells phase (A.D. 1250-1400) village of several acres, with at least one mound of abundant trash and subsurface deposition. The densest materials were south of the road to Cowlic, approximately 0.8 mile west of the Osborne store. The present condition of this site is not known, and its exact position relative to the cells has not been verified.

Based on the extent and density of materials and on the presence of cultural deposits in trash mounds, this village site can add abundant data on Sells phase occupation of the Papagueria. In view of the fact that no large Sells phase sites have been excavated in the Sells area since the 1930s, and since there have been major subsequent changes in archaeological methods, this village site is especially significant.

The cells are located in an archaeologically sensitive area that may contain at least one highly significant prehistoric site. Because of the proximity of the cells to the wash, additional buried cultural materials may exist in the vicinity.

A casual inspection of the area around the cells by Debowski and Coe indicated that much of the area is relatively unaffected by recent ground disturbance. Intact surface sites may, therefore, still exist in the vicinity of the cells.

The vicinity of the cells is characterized by a high probability of archaeological resources and a relative lack of recent disturbance. A high degree of disturbance is expected in the construction of new cells. It is recommended, therefore, that the locations for new cells, pipelines and related buildings be intensively surveyed for archaeological sites prior to any activities. This recommendation also applies to the 30 to 40 feet of pipeline to be relaid between Manhole A-1 and the junction box at the cells. If the effluent is at some later date used for irrigation, it is further recommended that any areas affected by irrigation or related construction also be surveyed early in the planning stages for such an undertaking. Because of the possibility of buried sites near Sells Wash, it is recommneded that an archaeologist monitor any earth moving operations related to the expansion or improvement of the effluent cells.

New Sewer Lines in the Housing Subdivision and in Isolated Lots

Within the housing subdivision in Sells, new sewer lines will be constructed from the houses to the existing main pipeline feeder. This area is expected to be affected by trenching and heavy equipment traffic.

Doelle and Brew (1976), archaeologists for ASM, surveyed the housing subdivision parcel in Sells. This area was bounded on the east by the foothills extending from the Artesa Mountains, and on the south by Main Street and its dirt road extensions. On the west the parcel is bounded by a north-south road on the east side of Lot 7 (the lot numbers shown on Papago Tribal Utilities Authority map), and a north-south fence extending from the dirt road to Route 86. On the north the parcel boundary is a line parallel to, and approximately 100 feet south of, Route 86. They also surveyed a group of four lots extending southward from the main parcel. These lots lie between two unsurveyed extensions where water and erosion control work is planned.

Doelle and Brew surveyed 28 isolated housing lots in Sells for cultural resources. There are discrepancies between their base map, drafted by Phoenix Western Engineers, Inc., and the base map drafted from aerial photographs, provided by STRAAM Engineers, Inc. (Appendix B). New lots were added after the survey was completed. Because of map discrepancies and planning changes, there are 11 isolated housing lots that have not been surveyed. These are listed in Appendix C. Surveyed areas are shown in Figure 2, deleted from most copies of this report. A map indicating housing lots in Sells is on file at the Cultural Resource Management Section of the Arizona State Museum.

Within the main housing subdivision parcel, Doelle and Brew noted scattered prehistoric and historic materials; owing to heavy 20th century surface disturbance, however, they determined that these were not of sufficient density or integrity to warrant site status. Within the parcel, materials were denser in the eastern quarter just below the extension of the Artesa Mountains.

The surveyed isolated lots did not contain prehistoric sites, although scattered prehistoric and historic artifacts were noted. Isolated Lot 12 (102) may be in the vicinity of AZ DD:1:29, a Hohokam site buried by some 75 cm of alluvium, but the location of this prehistoric site is in question. Buried sites also occur along the Sells-Gu Oidak road (PIR 24) and trenches in this area may reveal buried cultural materials.

The subdivision parcel and isolated housing lots exhibit varying degrees of recent soil disturbance. With the exception of Lot 5 (103) and the two nearby unnumbered lots, the isolated lots and the main subdivision parcel are within 0.5 mile of Sells Wash or Little Tucson Wash, the areas previously identified as archaeologically sensitive.

Monitoring of new pipeline trenches within the surveyed main subdivision parcel and within surveyed isolated lots is recommended. Survey prior to land modification and monitoring during construction are recommended for two areas: (1) land south of the subdivision where water and erosion control modifications are planned, and (2) the remaining unsurveyed and discrepant housing lots.

Retrofitting the Existing Lift Station

Significant additional ground disturbance is not now anticipated as a result of retrofitting the lift station. Archaeological survey and monitoring are, therefore, not recommended. If, at a later date, it is found that modifications will affect undisturbed soil around or beneath the lift station, it is recommended that construction be monitored by an archaeologist.

Long-term Planning Recommendations for Project Area Archaeological Resources

Federal legislation requires that the effects on archaeological resources be considered in any major undertaking receiving federal funding, subject to federal license or on federal land. Archaeological contract projects have been undertaken in the Sells area previously; future federally funded development will require additional studies.

Several sensitive areas within the project boundaries are identified in Chapter 6. An additional comparatively undisturbed area north of Sells Wash and south of an east-west line through Etoi Ki has not been surveyed but is believed to be suitable for ak chin farming; it is likely, therefore, to contain numerous archaeological resources.

In view of the archaeological sensitivity of the project area and the likelihood of future federally funded undertakings, a complete inventory of the project area is viewed as more effective for planning purposes than piecemeal, project-specific archaeological studies, for the following reasons. First, a complete inventory should, in the long run, minimize development costs and delays. With such an inventory locations for developments could be selected early in the planning stages to avoid significant cultural resources, thereby minimizing both the need for costly data recovery and the likelihood of project delays. Second, an accurate inventory of cultural resources would also decrease the chances of inadvertent duplicate survey coverage. Third, a complete inventory would provide a baseline against which the relative significance of specific cultural resources could be more accurately evaluated. Last, an inventory would also be valuable for purely archaeological considerations. Specific archaeological resources can only be partially understood if they are viewed as isolated phenomena rather than as parts of functioning regional systems. That larger areal surveys have generally yielded a deeper understanding of the past than have linear surveys or surveys of small parcels attests to the importance of a regional context for cultural resources. A complete inventory of the project area would be a significant step in providing this vital regional context, and in insuring that the research potential of resources in the project area is fully tapped.

It is strongly recommended that an intensive survey of the project area be undertaken to provide a complete inventory of cultural resources within its boundaries. The inventory survey could readily be staged in accordance with specific archaeological and development priorities. While it is beyond the scope of this assessment to identify all these priorities in detail, at least two general survey areas deserve high priority: (1) locations planned for development or construction in the near future, and (2) the unsurveyed area between Sells Wash and an east-west line through Etoi Ki, for which archaeological data are lacking.

Let us briefly review the conclusions of this chapter. It has been stated that natural and human disturbances outside the town of Sells are not likely to have seriously diminished the integrity of the archaeological record as a whole; within the town of Sells heavy surface disturbance undoubtedly has altered the archaeological record for surface sites, but subsurface materials may be intact. Survey and monitoring recommendations are offered for a series of proposed improvements in the Sells wastewater facilities. Finally, an intensive survey of the project area to provide a complete inventory of archaeological resources is recommneded as the most effective tool for long range planning in the project area.

Concluding Statement

This assessment identifies the area surrounding Sells as a rich gathering zone, in which a high density of prehistoric and historic cultural resources is expected. The 18 previously recorded sites in the project area provide an almost continuous record of occupation for the last 1,200 years and indicate a wide range of functions, from limited

activity areas to large villages. Consequently, the project area has the
potential to contribute to many problems pertinent to prehistory and history
on the Papaguería. Within the project area, piecemeal survey coverage has
not provided a complete inventory of cultural resources. A program of
survey and monitoring is recommended for specific improvements planned
for the Sells wastewater facilities. An intensive survey of the remaining
unsurveyed portions of the project area is seen as the most effective
means of providing a complete inventory, which can be used for long range
planning purposes.

REFERENCES

Antevs, Ernst
   1955   Geologic-climatic dating in the west. <u>American Antiquity</u>
            20(4):317-35.

   1959   Geological age of the Lehner Mammoth Site. <u>American</u>
            <u>Antiquity</u> 25(1):31-34.

Betancourt, Julio L.
   1978   An archaeological synthesis of the Tucson Basin: Focus
            on the Santa Cruz and its riverpark. <u>Arizona State</u>
            <u>Museum Archaeological Series</u> 116.

Bohrer, Vorsila
   1970   Ethnobotanical aspects of Snaketown, a Hohokam village
            in southern Arizona. <u>American Antiquity</u> 35(4): 413-30.

Breternitz, David A.
   1957   A brief archaeological survey of the lower Gila River.
            <u>Kiva</u> 22(2 and 3):1-13.

Brown, Douglas R.
   1976   Memorandum dated 3/31/76 to Chief, Division of External
            Archeological Programs, Western Archeological Center,
            National Park Service, Tucson. Trip report to Papago
            Indian Reservation.

Brown, Patricia Eyring
   1976   An archaeoloigcal survey of the Vaiva Vo to Kohatk Road,
            Papago Indian Reservation, southern Arizona. Office of
            Cultural Resource Management, Department of Anthropology,
            Arizona State University, Tempe.

Bryan, Kirk
   1925   The Papago country, Arizona. <u>United States Geological</u>
            <u>Survey Water-Supply Paper</u> 449.

Canouts, Veletta, Edward Germeshausen and Robert Larkin
   1972   An archaeological survey of the Santa Rosa Wash Project.
            <u>Arizona State Museum Archaeological Series</u> 18.

Castetter, Edward F. and Willis H. Bell
   1942   Pima and Papago Indian agriculture. <u>Inter-Americana Studies</u> 1.
            Albuquerque: University of New Mexico Press.

Clotts, H.V.
    1915   Report on nomadic Papago surveys. Report submitted to
            Superintendent of Irrigation, United States Indian
            Service, Department of Interior. On file at the Arizona
            State Museum, The University of Arizona, Tucson.

Curriden, Nancy T.
    n.d.a   Arizona T:16:41: A temporary-use activity site. Arizona
            State Museum Archaeological Series.

    n.d.b   AZ DD:1:21, Sells, Arizona: Mitigation of an ephemeral
            campsite with lithic chipping areas. MS. Cultural Resource
            Mamagement Section, Arizona State Museum, The University of
            Arizona, Tucson.

Danson, Edward B.
    1946   An archaeological survey of the Santa Cruz River Valley from
            the headwaters to the town of Tubac in Arizona. MS. Master's
            thesis, The University of Arizona, Tucson.

Debowski, Sharon S., Anique George, Richard Goddard, and Deborah Mullon
    1976   An archaeological survey of the Buttes Reservoir. Arizona
            State Museum Archaeological Series 93.

DiPeso, Charles C.
    1953   The Sobaipuri Indians of the upper San Pedro River Valley,
            southeastern Arizona. The Amerind Foundation 6,
            Dragoon.

    1956   The upper Pima of San Cayetano del Tumacacori: An archaeological
            reconstruction of the Ootam of Pimeria Alta. The Amerind
            Foundation 7, Dragoon.

    1968   Casas Grandes and the Gran Chichimeca. El Palacio 75:45-61.

Doelle, William H. and Susan A. Brew
    1976   An archaeological survey of proposed housing locations in
            Sells and Vaya Chin, Papago Indian Reservation, Arizona.
            Arizona State Museum Archaeological Series 107.

Doyel, David E.
    1974   Excavations in the Escalante Ruin Group, southern Arizona.
            Arizona State Museum Archaeological Series 37.

    1977a   Excavations in the middle Santa Cruz River Valley, southeastern
            Arizona. Arizona State Museum Contributions to Highway
            Salvage Archaeology in Arizona 44.

    1977b   Rillito and Rincon period settlement systems in the middle
            Santa Cruz River Valley: Alternative models. Kiva 43(2):
            93-110.

Ezell, Paul H.
1954 An archaeological survey of northwestern Papaguería. <u>Kiva</u> 19(2-4):1-26.

1955 The archaeological delineation of a cultural boundary in Papaguería. <u>American Antiquity</u> 20(4) part 1:367-74.

1963a The Maricopas. An identification from documentary sources. <u>Anthropological Papers of the University of Arizona</u> 6.

1963b Is there a Hohokam-Pima culture continuum? <u>American Antiquity</u> 29(1):61-66.

Ferg, Alan and Lawrence E. Vogler
1977 An archaeological survey of Route PIR 21: Kom Vo to Papago Farms, Papago Indian Reservation, Arizona. <u>Arizona State Museum Archaeological Series</u> 110.

Fontana, Bernard L.
1964 Report before the Indian Claims Commission, Docket No. 345, The Papago Tribe of Arizona vs. The United States of America. On file at the Arizona State Museum Library, The University of Arizona, Tucson.

1965 An archaeological site survey of the Cabeza Prieta Game Range, Arizona. MS. Arizona State Museum, The University of Arizona, Tucson.

Frick, Paul S.
1954 An archaeological survey in the Central Santa Cruz Valley, southern Arizona. MS. Master's thesis, The University of Arizona, Tucson.

Gladwin, Harold S. and Winifred Gladwin
1929a The red-on-buff culture of the Gila Basin. <u>Medallion Papers</u> 3.

1929b The red-on-buff culture of the Papaguería. <u>Medallion Papers</u> 4.

1930 The western range of the red-on-buff culture. <u>Medallion Papers</u> 5.

Gladwin, Harold S., Emil W. Haury, E.B. Sayles, and Nora Gladwin
1937 Excavations at Snaketown: I. Material culture. <u>Medallion Papers</u> 25. Reprinted by The University of Arizona Press, Tucson.

Goodyear, Albert C.
1975 Hecla II and III: An interpretive study of archaeological remains from the Lakeshore Project, Papago Reservation, south central Arizona. <u>Arizona State University Anthropological Research Paper</u> 9.

Granger, Byrd Howell
  1960   Will C. Barnes' Arizona place names. Tucson: The University
          of Arizona Press.

Grebinger, Paul Franklin
  1971   Hohokam cultural development in the middle Santa Cruz Valley,
          Arizona. Doctoral dissertation, Department of Anthropology,
          The University of Arizona, and University Microfilms, Ann
          Arbor, Michigan.

Greenleaf, J. Cameron
  1975a   Excavations at Punta de Agua. Anthropological Papers of the
          University of Arizona 26.

  1975b   The Fortified Hill Site near Gila Bend, Arizona. Kiva
          40(4): 213-82.

Hackenberg, Robert A.
  1962   Economic alternatives in arid lands: A case study of the Pima
          and Papago Indians. Ethnology 1(2):186-96.

  1964   Aboriginal land use and occupancy of the Papago Indians.
          MS. Master's thesis, The University of Arizona, Tucson.

Haury, Emil W.
  1950   The stratigraphy and archaeology of Ventana Cave. Tucson:
          The University of Arizona Press.

  1965   Snaketown: 1964-1965. Kiva 31(1):1-13.

  1975   Preface 1975. The stratigraphy and archaeology of Ventana
          Cave. Tucson: The University of Arizona Press.

  1976   The Hohokam: Desert farmers and craftsmen. Excavations at
          Snaketown 1964-1965. Tucson: The University of Arizona
          Press.

Hayden, Carl
  1965   A history of the Pima Indians and the San Carlos Irrigation
          Project. 89th Congress, 1st session, Senate Document 11,
          Washington.

Hayden, Julian D.
  1957   Excavations, 1940, at University Indian Ruin, Tucson, Arizona.
          Southwestern Monument Association Technical Series 5.

  1967   A summary history and prehistory of the Sierra Pinacate,
          Sonora. American Antiquity 32(3):335-44.

  1970   Of Hohokam origins and other matters. American Antiquity
          35(1):87-93.

Hayden, Julian D. (continued)
    1972   Hohokam petroglyphs of the Sierra Pinacate, Sonora and the
            Hohokam shell expeditions. _Kiva_ 37(2): 74-83.

    1976   Pre-Altithermal archaeology in the Sierra Pinacate, Sonora,
            Mexico. _American Antiquity_ 41(3): 274-89.

Hinton, Richard J.
    1970   _The hand-book to Arizona: Its resources, history,
            towns, mines, ruins and scenery._ First published in
            1878, Rio Grande Press, Glorieta.

Hinton, Thomas
    1955   A survey of the archaeological sites in the Altar Valley,
            Sonora. _Kiva_ 21(1 and 2): 1-12.

Huntington, Ellsworth
    1914   The climatic factor as illustrated in arid America.
            Carnegie Institute of Washington Publication 192.
            Washington, D.C.

Johnson, Alfred E.
    1963   The Trincheras culture of northern Sonora. _American
            Antiquity_ 29(2):174-86.

Jones, Bruce
    1974   Gu Vo Project--Papago Indian Reservation, preliminary
            report. MS. Western Archeological Center, National
            Park Service, Tucson.

Kelly, Isabel T.
    1978   The Hodges Ruin: A Hohokam community in the Tucson Basin.
            Anthropological Papers of the University of Arizona 30.
            Tucson: The University of Arizona Press.

King, Thomas J., Jr.
    1977   An archaeological survey of some horsetrails in Saguaro
            National Monument. MS. Western Archeological Center,
            National Park Service, Tucson.

Linford, Laurance D.
    n.d.   Archaeological interpretation through lithic analysis:
            Arizona AA:15:11. _Arizona State Museum Archaeological
            Series._

Lowe, Charles H.
    1964   Arizona's natural environment. Tucson: The University of
            Arizona Press.

Mark, Albyn K.
    1960   Excerpts from "Description of and variables relating to
            ecological change in the history of the Papago Indian
            population." Defense Exhibit 32 in Robert A. Hackenberg,
            1964, Aboriginal land use and occupancy of the Papago Indians.
            MS. Arizona State Museum, The University of Arizona, Tucson.

Masse, W. Bruce
    in   Excavations at Gu Achi: A reappraisal of Hohokam settlement
    prep.   and subsistence in the Arizona Papaguería. Western
            Archeological Center, National Park Service, Tucson.

McClellan, Carole and Lawrence E. Vogler
    1977   An archaeological assessment of Luke Air Force Range, located
            in Southwestern Arizona. Arizona State Museum Archaeological
            Series 113.

McDonald, James A., David A. Phillips, Jr., Yvonne Stewart, and Ric Windmiller
    1974   An archaeological survey of the Tucson Gas & Electric
            El Sol-Vail transmission line. Arizona State Museum Arch-
            aeological Series 53.

McGuire, Randall and Linda Mayro
    1978   Papago Wells Project: Archaeological surveys near Kaka and
            Stoa Pitk, the Papago Reservation, Arizona. Arizona State
            Museum Archaeological Series 120.

Raab, Mark L.
    1974   Archaeological investigations for the Santa Rosa Wash Project,
            Phase I preliminary report. Arizona State Museum Archaeological
            Series 60.

Rogers, Malcolm J.
    1936   Yuman pottery making. San Diego Museum Papers 2.

    1939   Early lithic industries of the lower basin of the Colorado
            River and adjacent desert areas. San Diego Museum Papers 3.

    1945   An outline of Yuman prehistory. Southwestern Journal of
            Anthropology 1(2):167-98.

    1958   San Dieguito implements from the terraces of the Rincon-
            Pantano and Rillito drainage system. Kiva 24(1): 1-23.

    1966   Ancient hunters of the far west. San Diego: The Union-
            Tribune Publishing Company.

Rosenthal, E. Jane
    n.d.   AZ AA:13:21: A prehistoric activity area near modern
            Comobabi village. MS. Western Archeological Center,
            National Park Service, Tucson.

Rosenthal, E. Jane, Douglas R. Brown, Marc Severson, and John B. Clonts
    1978   The Quijotoa Valley Project. Cultural Resources
            Management Division, Western Archeological Center, National
            Park Service, Tucson.

Sauer, C.O. and Donald Brand
    1931   Prehistoric settlements of Sonora with specific reference
            to Cerros de Trincheras. University of California
            Publications in Geography 5(3):67-148.

Sayles, E.B. and Ernst Antevs
    1941   The Cochise culture. Medallion Papers 29.

Scantling, Frederick H.
    1940   Excavations at the Jackrabbit Ruin, Papago Indian Reservation,
            Arizona. MS. Master's thesis, Department of Anthropology,
            The University of Arizona, Tucson.

Schroeder, Albert H.
    1952   A brief survey of the lower Colorado River from Davis
            Dam to the international border. U.S. Bureau of Reclamation,
            Reproduction Unit, Region Three, Boulder City, Nevada.

    1957   The Hakataya cultural tradition. American Antiquity 23(2):
            176-78.

    1960   The Hohokam, Sinagua and the Hakataya. Archives of Archaeology 5.
            Society for American Archaeology and the University of Wisconsin
            Press, Madison.

    1961   An archaeological survey of the Painted Rocks Reservoir,
            western Arizona. Kiva 27(1):1-27.

    1964   Comments on Johnson's "The Trincheras culture of northern Sonora."
            American Antiquity 30(1):104-06.

    1967   Comments on "Salvage archaeology in the Painted Rock Reservoir,
            western Arizona." Arizona Archaeology 1:1-10.

Shenk, Lynette O. and Peter D. Coston
    n.d.   An archaeological mitigation of site AZ AA:14:14, Papaguería,
            southeastern Arizona. Arizona State Museum Archaeological
            Series.

Shreve, Forrest and Ira L. Wiggins
    1964   Vegetation and flora of the Sonoran Desert, Vol. 1. Stanford:
            Stanford University Press.

Somers, Gary F.
    1975   Archeological survey investigation: Papago Indian Reservation.
            MS. Western Archeological Center, National Park Service,
            Tucson.

Spain, James Nicholas
    1975   Lithic Analysis: Arizona T:11:31 (ASM) and AA:10:3 (ASM):
            A structural model. Arizona State Museum Archaeological
            Series 86.

Spier, Leslie
    1933   Yuman tribes of the Gila River. Chicago: University of Chicago
            Press.

Stacy, Valeria Kay Pheriba
    1973   Final report, archeological surveys of FY 73, BIA Road
            Projects. MS. Western Archeological Center, National
            Park Service, Tucson.

    1974   Cerros de Trincheras in the Arizona Papaguería. Doctoral
            dissertation, Department of Anthropology, The University
            of Arizona, Tucson.

    1975   Archaeological survey in the Arizona Papaguería. Kiva 40(3):
            181-87.

Steen, Charlie R.
    1965   Excavations in Compound A, Casa Grande National Monument,
            1963. Kiva 31(2):59-82.

Stewart, Yvonne and Lynn S. Teague
    1974   An ethnoarchaeological study of the Vekol Copper Mining Project.
            Arizona State Museum Archaeological Series 49.

STRAAM Engineers, Inc.
    1978   Facility plan for Sells, Arizona, C-04-0233, Draft 1, October
            1978. MS on file at the Cultural Resource Management Section,
            Arizona State Museum, The University of Arizona, Tucson.

Teague, Lynn S.
    1976   Letter report dated 11/1/76 to Mrs. Irene Wallace, Chairperson,
            Executive Health Staff, Papago Tribe of Arizona, Sells, Arizona,
            in reference to an archaeological survey of a proposed health
            services complex in Sells, Arizona. On file, Cultural Resource
            Management Section, Arizona State Museum, The University of
            Arizona, Tucson.

Underhill, Ruth M.
    1939   Social organization of the Papago Indians. Columbia University
            Contributions to Anthropology 30.

U.S. Army Corps of Engineers, Los Angeles District, California
    1976   Flood plain information, Sells Wash and tributary, vicinity
            of Sells, Papago Indian Reservation, Arizona. On file,
            Cultural Resource Management Section, Arizona State Museum,
            The University of Arizona, Tucson.

Van Devender, Thomas R.
    1973   Late Pleistocene plants and animals of the Sonoran Desert:
            A survey of ancient packrat middens in southwestern Arizona.
            Doctoral dissertation, The University of Arizona, Tucson.

    1977   Holocene woodlands in the southwestern deserts. Science 198:
            189-92.

Vivian, R. Gwinn
    1965   An archaeological survey of the lower Gila River, Arizona.
            Kiva 30(4):95-146.

Vogler, Lawrence E.
    1978   Reports on data recovery operations at two sites in the
            Papago Indian Reservation, Arizona: Sonora C:3:2 and Arizona
            Z:14:47. Arizona State Museum Archaeological Series 119.

Wagoner, J.J.
    1952   History of the cattle industry in southern Arizona, 1540-
            1940. University of Arizona Social Science Bulletin 20.

Wasley, William W.
    1960   A Hohokam platform mound at the Gatlin Site, Gila Bend,
            Arizona. American Antiquity 26(2):244-62.

Wasley, William W.
    1966   Classic period Hohokam. MS. Arizona State Museum, The University
            of Arizona, Tucson.

Wasley, William W. and Alfred E. Johnson
    1961   Hohokam archaeology of the Painted Rocks Reservoir
            area near Gila Bend, western Arizona. MS. Arizona State
            Museum, The University of Arizona, Tucson.

    1965   Salvage archaeology in Painted Rocks Reservoir, western
            Arizona. Anthropological Papers of the University of Arizona 9.

Withers, Arnold M.
    1941   Excavations at Valshni Village, Papago Indian Reservation, Arizona.
            MS. Master's thesis, Department of Anthropology, The University
            of Arizona, Tucson.

Yablon, Ronald K.
    1978   Archeological Investigations on Vaiva Vo-Kohatk Road Project,
            Papago Indian Reservation. Office of Cultural Resource
            Management, Department of Anthropology, Arizona State
            University, Tempe.

APPENDIX B

Isolated Housing Lots Surveyed
by Doelle and Brew (1976)

Isolated Lot Number on Project Map Used by Doelle and Brew (1976)	Owner [from Doelle and Brew (1976)]	Lot Number Listed on P.T.U.A. Map as of October 1978	Lot Number Listed on Housing Authority Map as of October 1979
1	Max Chavez	---*	---
2	Robert Price	---	---
3	Manny Royle	---	---
4	Deer Kennedy	---	---
5	Thomas Rivas	---	---
6	Felix Norris	---	---
7	Ella Rae Thomas	9	107
8	Paul Norris	8	105
9	Larry Garcia	7	109
10	Virginia Parvello	---	---
11	Angelita Muldonado	---	---
12	Howard Mendez	---	---
13	Daniel Jose, Lucas Francisco	---	---
14	George Ignacio	---	---
15	Sarah Patrick	---	---
16	Ernie Antone	3	108
17	Fernando Cruz	---	---
18	Alexander Gonzales	10	104
19	George Miguel	---	---
20	Juan Mattais	---	---
21	Enos Francisco, Jr.	---	---
22	Alex Francisco	2	101
23	Nyla Antone	---	---
24	Unknown	---	---
25	Nathan Andre	---	---
26	Renaldo Miguel	---	---
27	Floyd Jaquin	---	---
28	Lorin Patricio May be same as	5	103
In subdivision	Unknown	1	36
In extension of subdivision	Unknown	11	112

*---signifies no corresponding number on P.T.U.A. or Housing Authority maps

APPENDIX C

Unsurveyed Isolated Housing Lots

Location	Unnumbered Lots	Lot Number on Papago Tribal Utilities Authority Map	Lot Number On Housing Authority Map
A. North of Route 86	1. proposed Housing Authority building across from Housing Authority offices now in use		
	4. unnumbered lot north of Route 86 approximately 600 feet east of the intersection between Route 86 and the road to Topawa	2. Lot 6 3. Lot 13	Lot 111 Lot 106
B. South of Route 86	5. unnumbered lot approximately 120 feet southwest of the Catholic Church	6. Lot 4* 7. Lot 12* 8. Lot 5*	Lot 110 Lot 102 Lot 103
	9. & 10. 2 unnumbered lots* approximately 800 feet WNW of Lot 5 (103) and one approximately 700 feet NNW of Lot 5 (103)		
C. South of PIR 24 (Sells to Gu Oidak)		11. Lot 14	Lot 100

*These lots may have been surveyed by Doelle and Brew but this is uncertain because of discrepancies between maps.